스포츠 잉글리시
Sports English

전유섭 지음

가림출판사

Preface

We are very happy to publish this book which is necessary for the students who are majoring in the physical education.

Today we extended upon the 21C, and it can not be too much to emphasize the necessity of obtaining intelligence through the internet.

In this globalized world, it will be a great help to the individual success and the national development to keep a good understanding freely with others and to get the technical knowledge in each field of specialization and put it to practical use, not excepting the physical educators.

This book, SPORTS ENGLISH, is written in English in order to improve your command of English, I hope you will make a great progress in reading comprehension ability as well as in your field of specialization.

We extend our gratitude for his help and to president Kang, Sun-Hee of GALIM Publishing Co.

2009. 2

From the Author

CONTENTS

CHAPTER 1
Physical education

What is philosophy?

Philosophy is a field of inquiry[1] that attempts to help individuals evaluate[2], in a satisfying and meaningful manner, their relationships[3] to the universe[4]. Philosophy seeks to help people evaluate themselves and their world by giving them a basis with which to deal with the problems of life and death, good and evil, freedom and restraint[5], beauty and ugliness[6]. Aristotle[7] said that philosophy is the grouping of the knowledge of the universals. A dictionary definition reports that it is the love of wisdom, the science that investigates[8] the facts and principles of reality and of human nature and conduct. Copleston writes: "Philosophy...is rooted in the desire to understand the world, in the desire to find an intelligible[9] pattern[10] in events and to answer problems which occur to the mind in connection[11] with the

---

1) inquiry - n. 문의, 조사, 연구, 탐구
2) evaluate - vt. 평가하다, 가치를 검토하다
3) relationship - n. 관계, 관련
4) universe - n. 우주, 만유, 만물
5) restraint - n. 제지, 금지, 억제
6) ugliness - a. 추한, 보기싫은, 못생긴
7) Aristotle - n. 그리스의 철학자(B. C. 384 - 322)
8) investigate - v. 조사하다, 연구하다, 심사하다
9) intelligible - a. 이해할 수 있는, 알기 쉬운, 명료한
10) pattern - n. 모범, 본보기; 본, 모형, 원형; 형, 양식
11) connection - n. 관계, 관련; 연결, 결합

world."

In defining the word philosophy Webster says: "Love of wisdom means the desire to search for the real facts and values in life and in the universe, and to evaluate and interpret these with an unbiased[12] and unprejudiced[13] mind." As can be seen from these definitions, philosophy offers an explanation of life and the principles that guide human lives. To comprehend[14] more clearly the meaning of philosophy, one should briefly examine the major components[15] of which philosophy is composed.

Metaphysics

Metaphysics[16] is associated with the principles of being. This component attempts to answer a series of related questions: What is the meaning of existence[17]? What is real? How are human actions governed? How and why did the universe evolve[18]? What is the nature of God? The question: What experiences in the physical education

---

12) unbiased - a. 편견이 없는, 공평한
13) unprejudiced - a. 편견이 없는, 선입관이 없는, 편파적이 아닌, 공정한
14) comprehend - vt. 이해하다, 파악하다, 깨닫다
15) component - a. 구성하고 있는, 성분을 이루는 n. 성분, 구성요소
16) Metaphysics - n. 철학; 형이상학
17) existence - n. 존재, 실재, 현존
18) evolve - vt. 발전시키다; 전개하다; 진화하다

program will better enable students to meet the challenges[19] of the real world? is metaphysical in nature[20].

Will Durant, a contemporary[21] philosopher, says that metaphysics investigates the reality of everything concerned with human beings and the universe.

Epistemology

Epistemology[22] is concerned with methods of obtaining knowledge and the kinds of knowledge that can be gained. It is a comprehensive study of knowledge that attempts to define the sources[23], authority[24], principles, limitations[25], and validity[26] of knowledge. In physical education we are concerned with knowledge regarding the role of physical activity and its impact on the physical, mental, emotional, and social development of individuals. We are seeking the truth about physical education, and epistemology seeks to answer the question: What is true?

---

19) challenge - n. 도전 v. ...에 도전하다
20) nature - n. 자연, 천지만물; 천성, 본성; 성질, 자질
21) contemporary - a. 동시대의, 동연대의, 그 당시의
22) Epistemology - n. 철학; 인식론
23) source - n. 근원, 근본, 원천
24) authority - n. 권위, 권력; 권한, 권능
25) limitation - n. 제한, 한정, 규제
26) validity - n. 정당성, 타당성

Axiology

Axiology[27] helps to determine to what use truth is to be put. It asks: How do we determine what has value, and on what criteria[28] is this judgement based?

Axiology is concerned with the aims and values of society and is extremely important in physical education because the aims and values set by society become the basis of the curriculum[29] used in schools and colleges. In physical education the following question must be answered: How can the values that society holds so dearly be embraced[30] in the physical education program? Our society holds dearly the value of "equality for all." We can see this value exemplified[31] by having students from all walks of life playing together and developing tolerance[32] for one another. Students who learn to respect[33] one another on the playing fields, it is hoped, will be more likely to carry those feelings off the field.

---

27) axiology - n. 철학; 가치론
28) criteria - n. 기준, 표준
29) curriculum - n. 교과과정, 이수과정
30) embrace - v. 얼싸안다, 껴안다, 포옹하다
31) exemplify - vt. 예증(예시)하다
32) tolerance - n. 관용; 아량, 포용력, 도량
33) respect - vt. 존중하다, 존경하다

Ethics

Ethics[34] is a more individualized and personalized subdivision[35] of axiology. It helps to define moral character[36] and serves as a basis for an individual code of conduct. Ethics attempts to answer the question:

What is the highest standard of behavior each person should strive[37] to attain? The strengthening of moral conduct is an important function of physical education. In physical education the following questions must be answered: How can games and sports be utilized[38] to help the individual learn right conduct? Is character education through physical education possible? Physical education places individuals in situations that reveal their true nature and character. One who plays on a team may soon realize that using "four-letter words"[39] is not acceptable. The student who plays by the "rules" and acts like a "sportsman" at all times will win the respect of fellow teammates. The relationships formed in physical education and the character that is developed, it is hoped, will carry over to behavioral situations[40] occurring out of school.

---

34) ethics – n. 윤리학, 도덕론
35) subdivision – n. 재분, 잘게 나눔, 세분
36) character – n. 특성, 특성, 인격, 성격, 품성
37) strive – vi. 노력하다, 얻으려고 애쓰다
38) utilize – vt. 활용하다, 소용되게 하다
39) four-letter words – 네 글자로 된 추잡한 말
40) situation – n. 위치, 장소; 입장, 사정; 정세, 형세, 상태, 사태

Logic

Logic[41] seeks to provide us with a sound and intelligent method of living. Logic describes the steps that should be taken in thinking and puts ideas into an orderly, structured sequence[42] that leads to accurate thinking.

It helps to set up standards by which the accuracy[43] of ideas may be measured. Logic concerns itself with the orderly connection of one fact or idea with another. It asks the question: What method of reasoning will lead to the truth? Physical educators must use logical thought processes in arriving[44] at the truth. When students ask questions such as: "Why should I play football?" the physical education teacher must not answer by saying: "Because it's in the program." The teacher should explain in clear reasoning the benefits[45] that can be derived from playing football, since only then will the student really understand its true value.

---

41) logic - n. 논리학
42) sequence - n. 결과, 귀추; 결론; 연속, 계속
43) accuracy - n. 정확, 정밀, 정밀도
44) arrive - vi. 도착하다, (어떤 결론, 확신 따위에) 도달하다
45) benefit - n. 이익, 이득(상업)

Esthetics

Esthetics[46] is the study and determination[47] of criteria for beauty in nature and the arts, including dance, drama, sculpture[48], painting, music, and writing. Esthetics, which is a less scientific branch of axiology, is concerned not only with art but also with the artist and the appreciation[49] of what he has created.

In an attempt to determine the close relationship of art to nature, esthetics asks the question: What is beauty? There is esthetics appreciation involved in watching a gymnast[50] perform on the trampoline[51], a football player leap[52] high to catch a pass, or a baseball player dive to catch a line drive, just as there is an esthetics appreciation gained from viewing great works of art or listening to a symphony[53] orchestra. The physical movements that one can view in athletics[54] are often a source of great pleasure.

The components known as metaphysics, epistemology, axiology, ethics, logic, and esthetics represent aspects of

---

46) esthetics – n. 미학
47) determination – n. 결의, 결심, 결단력; 결정
48) sculpture – n. 조각(술), 조각품
49) appreciation – n. 평가, 판단, 이해
50) gymnast – n. 체육교사, 체육(전문)가
51) trampoline – n. 탄성을 이용한 도약용 운동기구
52) leap – vi. 껑충 뛰다, 뛰어 오르다, 도약하다
53) symphony – n. 교향곡, 심포니; (회화) 색채의 조화
54) athletics – n. 운동경기

philosophy. In developing a philosophy for any particular[55] field, one would turn for information to each of these areas. These components would be applied in formulating a philosophy for any particular field within the educational endeavor[56], such as in health, physical education, or recreation. Philosophy yields[57] a comprehensive understanding of reality, which, when applied to education or any other field of interest, gives direction that would likely be lacking[58] otherwise.

Philosophy and physical education

In today's changing society[59], there must be a sound[60] philosophy of physical education for our profession to survive[61] in the present educational system. Physical

---

55) particular - a. 특별한, 특유의, 특수한
56) endeavor - vt. 애쓰다, ...하려고 노력하다 n. 노력, 진력; 시도
57) yield - vi. 생기게 하다, 산출하다; (이익 따위를) 가져오다
58) lack - n. 부족, 결핍 vi. 결핍하다, 모자라다
59) society - n. 사회, (사회) 집단; 세상
60) sound - n. 소리, 음, 음향 vi. 소리가 나다, 소리를 내다
61) survive - vt. 살아남다, 생존하다

educators must ask themselves such important questions as: What has value in today's society? and What is relevant to the needs of today's students? We must discover the answer to these questions, and a philosophy will be the means to that end. A philosophy of physical education will serve the following functions.

A philosophy of physical education guides one's actions. To function as an intelligent[62] being, one needs a philosophy of life that will guide one's actions. One needs knowledge about what is right before any program can be created. A philosophy will help the teacher to decide what he or she wants to have happen to students in the gymnasium[63].

A philosophy of physical education provides[64] the direction[65] for the profession. Today in physical education many of the curriculums lack order and direction.

A philosophy of physical education will help to give direction to our programs. When assumptions[66] are made by the physical education teacher, for example, that physical education strengthens human relationships because children play together, they should be based on a system of

---

62) intelligent - a. 지성을 갖춘, 지적인, 영리한
63) gymnasium - n. 체육관, 실내 체육장; 고대 그리스의 연무장
64) provide - vt. 제공하다, 공급하다
65) direction - n. 지도, 지휘; 감독, 관리; 방향, 방위
66) assumption - n. 인수, 취임; 가정, 가설

reflective educational thinking that embraces logic and other philosophical components. A philosophy of physical education will help to provide this system.

A philosophy of physical education makes society aware[67] that physical education contributes[68] to its values. Physical education in the coming decades[69] is going to have to face that people are not going to be satisfied with only such statements as: "Students who participate in physical education show improvement in endurance." This is important, but it does not go far enough. In today's changing society, people want to know how physical education can contribute to the solution[70] of such problems as student unrest and how physical education programs can help stem the tide of racial discrimination[71]. A well-thought-through philosophy of physical education will assist in interpreting those values important in society so that programs can be established to help solve the problems plaguing[72] this nation.

A philosophy of physical education aids in bringing the members of the profession closer together. Many members

---

67) aware - a. (서술적) 깨닫고, 의식하고, 알고
68) contribute - vt. 공헌하다, 기여하다; (금품 따위를) 기부하다
69) decade - n. 십 년간; 열 개, 한 벌, 열 권
70) solution - n. 용해, 용해상태; (문제 등의) 해결, 해명
71) discrimination - n. 구별, 식별, 판별
72) plague - n. 역병, 전염병; 재앙, 저주, 천벌 vt. 역병(재앙 따위)에 걸리게 하다

of the physical education profession are dissatisfied with what they see happening in their field today. A philosophy of physical education will enable[73] physical educators to better determine how they can best contribute to mankind and to society and thus provide members of the profession the opportunity[74] to work together in making such a contribution.

A philosophy of physical eduction explains[75] the relationship between physical eduction and general education. A philosophy of physical education will help in the development of a rationale[76] showing that the field has objectives that are closely related to the objectives of general education. In the definition of physical education the importance of education "of and through the physical" is stressed. The goal, as in general education, is to develop the "whole" student. A philosophy of physical education that enunciates[77] the basic goals will give evidence that the profession has objectives that are related to the objectives of general education.

Physical educators must strive to develop their educational philosophies in a rational, logical, and

---

73) enable - vt. ...에게 힘(능력)을 주다, ...에게 가능성을 주다
74) opportunity - n. 기회, 호기
75) explain - vt. 분명하게 하다, 알기 쉽게 하다; 해석하다, 설명하다
76) rationale - n. 이론적 설명; 근본적 원리, 이유
77) enunciate - vt, vi. (학설 따위를) 발표하다; (이론, 제안 따위를) 선언하다

systematic manner and to represent[78] the best interests of all humans. This means that scientific facts must be assembled[79] and workable theories applied that support the worth of physical education as an important and necessary service to humanity[80].

Physical education-its meaning and philosophy

The word physical refers to the body. It is often used in reference[81] to various bodily characteristics[82] such as physical strength, physical development, physical prowess[83], physical health, and physical appearance[84].

It refers to the body as contrasted[85] to the mind. Therefore when the word education is added to the word

---

78) represent - vt. 묘사하다, 그리다; 설명하다, 말하다, 기술하다, 주장하다
79) assemble - vt. 모으다, 집합시키다; vi. 모이다, 회합하다
80) humanity - n. 인류; 인간성, 인간의 속성, 인간다움
81) reference - n. 참조, 참고; 참고문, 참고문헌
82) characteristic - n. 특징, 특질; 특성; a. 특질의, 특색을 이루는
83) prowess - n. 용감, 무용; 용감한 행위
84) appearance - n. 외관, 겉보기, 생김새; (외면적인) 형세, 정세, 상황
85) contrast - vt. 대조, 대비시키다

physical, thus forming the phrase[86] physical education, it refers to the process of education that concerns activities which develop and maintain the human body.

When an individual is playing a game, swimming, marching, working out on the parallel bars[87], skating, or performing in any one of the gamut[88] of physical education activities, education is taking place at the same time. This education may be conducive[89] to the enrichment of the individual' s life, or it may be detrimental[90].

It may be a satisfying experience, or it may be an unhappy one. It may help in the building of a strong and cohesive[91] society, or it may have antisocial[92] results for the participant[93]. Whether physical education helps or inhibits[94] the attainment of education objectives will depend to a great extent on the leadership responsible for its direction. Physical education is an important part of the educational process. It is not a frill or an ornament[95] tacked

---

86) phrase - n. (문법) 구; 말씨, 표현(법)
87) parallel bars - n. 평행봉 운동기구
88) gamut - n. (사물의) 전 범위, 전 영역
89) conducive - a. 도움이 되는, 이바지하는, 공헌하는
90) detrimental - a. 유해한, 손해되는
91) cohesive - a. 점착력이 있는; 밀착(결합)하는; (물리) 응집력이 있는
92) antisocial - a. 사회를 어지럽히는, 반사회적인
93) participant - a. 참여(관여)하는, 참가하는; n. 참여자, 참가자
94) inhibit - vt. 금하다; 방해하다, 억제하다
95) ornament - n. 꾸밈, 장식; 장식품, 장신구

on to the school program as a means of keeping children busy. It is, instead, a vital[96] part of education. Through a well-directed physical education program, children develop skills for the worthy use of leisure time, engage in activities conducive to healthful living, develop socially, and contribute to their physical and mental health.

A study of history reveals[97] that other civilizations[98] have recognized[99] the important place of physical education in the training of their youth. In ancient Athens, for example, three main subjects were studied by every Athenian: gymnastics, grammar, and music. Here in the United States the contributions of physical education to the educational program have been recognized for many years. In 1918 the National Educational Association[100] set forth its well-known Cardinal Principles of Secondary Education[101], which listed seven objectives of education: health, command of fundamental[102] processes, worthy home membership, vocation[103], citizenship[104], worthy use of leisure time, and

---

96) vital - a. 생생한, 생기가 넘치는: 절대로 필요한, 지극히 중요한

97) reveal - vt. (숨겨졌던 것을) 드러내다; 알리다, 누설하다, 폭로하다

98) civilization - n. 문명, 문화

99) recognize - vt. 알아보다, 보고 곧 알다; 인정하다

100) National Education Association - n. 미국교육협회

101) Cardinal Principles of Secondary Education - n. 중등교육의 기본원칙

102) fundamental - a. 기초의, 기본의, 근본적인

103) vocation - n. 직업, 생업, 장사, 일

104) citizenship - n. 시민권

ethical character. Physical education is playing an important part in achieving these objectives. As a result of such contributions as the benefits of exercise to physical health, the fundamental physical skills that make for a more interesting, efficient[105], and vigorous[106] life, and the social education that contributes to the development of character and good human relations, these cardinal principles are brought nearer to realization.

Terminology

The multiplicity[107] of terms that are sometimes used synonymously[108] for physical education makes it imperative that the meaning of these various terms be clarified[109].

Hygiene. Hygiene[110] comes from the Greek word

---

105) efficient - a. 능률적인, 효과적인
106) vigorous - a. 활발한, 박력 있는, 강건한
107) multiplicity - n. 다수, 중복; 다양성
108) synonymously - ad. 동의어의, 유의어의, 같은 뜻의
109) clarify - vt. (의미, 견해 따위를) 분명(명료)하게 하다, 해명하다
110) hygiene - n. 위생학

hygieinos, meaning healthful. It refers to the science of preserving one's health. Hygiene often refers to rules or principles prescribed[111] for the purpose of developing and maintaining health. In past years many school physical education departments were known as departments of hygiene; a few still use this term. It appears that the term became popular as a result of legislation[112] in various states that sought to have the effects of tobacco and alcohol[113] brought to the attention of[114] all students through a course often known by the name of hygiene. There are still many laws on the statute books[115] prescribing such instruction. Since World War I the term hygiene has become more or less obsolete. Newer terminology[116] is being used, such as health education and personal and community health.

Physical culture. The term physical culture[117] is obsolete[118] in education. It was used in the late nineteenth century to parallel names of other courses, such as religious

---

111) prescribe - vt. 규정하다, 지시하다, 명하다
112) legislation - n. 입법, 법률제정
113) tobacco and alcohol - n. 담배와 술
114) brought to the attention of - 주의를 환기시키다
115) statute book - n. 법령전서
116) terminology - n. 전문용어, 술어
117) physical culture - n. 체육문화
118) obsolete - a. 쇠퇴한, 시대에 뒤진, 진부한, 구식의

culture[119], social culture[120], and intellectual culture[121]. This term is still used by some faddists[122] in commercial ventures[123] to popularize[124] the beneficial effects of exercise. Individuals such as the late Bernarr Macfadden have, by means of their publications and business enterprises[125], done a great deal to spread[126] the use of such terminology.

Physical culture has been used synonymously for physical training. It implies that health may be promoted[127] through various physical activities. It is a term, however, that is not in use today in our schools.

Gymnastics. The word gymnastics refers to exercises that are adaptable to or are performed in a gymnasium. It is the art of performing various types of physical exercises and feats of skill[128]. The term has been and still is used extensively in the various physical education programs in

---

119) religious culture - n. 종교문화
120) social culture - n. 사회문화
121) intellectual culture - n. 지적문화
122) faddist - n. 변덕쟁이
123) commercial venture - n. 상기업
124) popularize - vt. 대중화하다; 보급시키다
125) enterprise - n. 기획, 계획; 기업체, 기업경영
126) spread - vt. 퍼트리다, 보급시키다; 펼치다, 전개하다
127) promote - vt. 진척시키다, 증진하다, 장려하다
128) feats of skill - 뛰어난 기술, 재주

Europe.

Anyone trained in physical education has heard mention of such programs as the German and Swedish systems of gymnastics. Formal drills such as calisthenics were utilized extensively in many physical education programs in the United States until recently. Today, when one thinks of gymnastics, what comes to mind[129] is formal drills[130] conducted either with or without the use of apparatus[131]. Americans do not use the term synonymously with physical education but, instead, with just that phase[132] of the physical education program concerned with formal drills. Physical education programs today are more concerned with allowing the individual to express himself or herself in various types of games rather than just in formal drill.

Physical training. The term physical training has a military tinge[133] to many individuals. It is a term that has been used in school programs of physical activity and also in the armed forces. Clark Hetherington used the term to connote[134] big-muscle activity[135] in the school program of physical

---

129) what comes to mind – 생각에 어떤 것이 떠오르다
130) formal drill – 형식적인 훈련
131) apparatus – n. (한 벌의) 장치, 기계, 기구
132) phase – n. (발달, 변화의) 단계, 국면
133) military tinge – n. 군대의 기미, 냄새
134) connote – vt. 내포하다
135) big-muscle activity – 대근근육의 활동

education.

On the other hand[136], during World War Ⅱ and at the present time, this term refers to the entire[137] program of physical conditioning that the armed forces require recruits[138] to go through as preparation for their rigorous duties. Most individuals agree that because of the military connection, the term is used to imply training the term has become rather outmoded[139] for the present physical education programs found in the public schools. Today, physical education programs realize outcomes other than just those concerned with the physical aspects. For example, there are sociological outcomes[140] that result in an individual's better adaptation to group living.

The term physical education also implies[141] that physical activity serves the field of eduction in a much broader sense than physical training does.

Fitness and physical fitness. A group of members of the American Association for Health, Physical Education, and Recreation approved the following definition of fitness: That

---

136) on the other hand - 한편
137) entire - a. 전체의; 완전한
138) recruit - n. 보충병, 신병
139) outmode - vt. vi. 유행에 뒤떨어지다
140) sociological outcome - 사회적인 성과
141) imply - vt. 함축하다, 암시하다

state which characterizes the degree to which the person is able to function. In other words, fitness represents the capacity[142] to live most vigorously and effectively with one's own resources.

Physical fitness refers primarily[143] to bodily aspects of fitness. It implies such abilities as that of resisting fatigue[144], performing with an acceptable[145] degree of motor ability, and being able to adapt to muscular stress.

Health. Health, according to the World Health Organization[146], refers to such qualities as physical, mental[147], emotional[148], and social health. It is not limited to the mere absence[149] of disease and infirmity[150]. It means total fitness.

Recreation. Recreation is concerned with those activities performed by an individual during hours not at work. It is frequently[151] referred to as leisure-time activity. Recreation

---

142) capacity - n. 능력, 재능
143) primarily - ad. 첫째로, 주로, 근본적으로
144) fatigue - n. 피로, 피곤
145) acceptable - a. 받아들일 수 있는
146) World Health Organization - 세계보건기구
147) mental - a. 정신의
148) emotional - a. 정서의, 감정의
149) absence - n. 부재, 결석, 결근
150) infirmity - n. 허약, 쇠약, 질환
151) frequently - ad. 종종, 때때로, 빈번히

education is aimed at teaching people to utilize their leisure hours in a constructive manner[152]. This implies a careful selection of activities.

Athletics. The term athletics refers to the games or sports that are usually engaged in by robust and skilled individuals. The interest in athletics in the United States has been largely inherited from Great Britain. With the introduction of athletics into colleges and universities, there has been a rapid growth in all sport engaged in on an intercollegiate basis[153].

Many lay persons[154] frequently think of athletics and physical education as being similar in meaning. However, most physical education personnel think of athletics as one phase of a broad physical education program- that division of the program concerned with interscholastic or intercollegiate[155] sports competition. The primary responsibility of a director of athletics in a school is the direction of this competitive program.

Sports Medicine. Dr. Neal Tremble of Drake University, a

---

152) in a constructive manner – 적극적인 방식으로
153) in on an intercollegiate basis – 상호 대학 간의 기초로
154) lay person – n. 문외한
155) interscholastic or intercollegiate – 초·중·고교 간의 혹은 대학 간의

Fellow in the American College of Sports Medicine, points out that the meaning of sports medicine involves the interprofessional[156] and interdisciplinary[157] implications of the following components:

Athletic medicine : 운동의학

Accident prevention : 사고예방

Evaluation and management of injuries : 상해의 관리와 평가

Traumatology : 외상학

Biomechanics : 생체역학

Anatomic analysis of movement : 운동의 해부학적 분석

Kinetic analysis of movement : 운동의 기능학적 분석

Clinical medicine : 임상의학

Clinical consequences of physical activity : 신체활동의 임상적 결과

Health appraisal of physical activity : 신체활동의 건강평가

Pharmacology : 약리학

Physical activity and health : 신체활동과 건강

Prescriptions of activity for patients : 환자들을 위한 활동의 처방

Therapy and rehabilitation : 치료와 재활

---

156) interprofessional - a. 직업 간의
157) interdisciplinary - a. 둘 이상 학문분야에 걸치는

Growth and development : 성장과 발달

Maturation and aging : 성숙과 노화

Physical anthropology : 자연 인류학

Tissue changes : 조직변화

Physiology : 생리학

Biochemistry of exercise : 운동생화학

Environmental influences : 환경의 영향

Human performance : 인간수행

Nutritional considerations : 영양의 요건

Pathophysiological conditions and exercise : 병리생리학적인 조건과 운동

Psychology and sociology : 심리학과 사회학

Behavior : 행동

Cybernetics : 인공두뇌학

Group dynamics : 집합역학

Motor learning : 운동학습

Perception : 지각

*참고 : The above contents trace a quotation to its original source from Charles A. Bucher's Foundations of physical education

CHAPTER 2
History of Taekwondo

From the traditional cultural heritage to a sport loved by the world

Taekwondo, which is a national martial art[1] of Korea, is one of the proudest[2] cultural heritages[3] for the Korean people. Taekwondo has been developed into a modern sport as a result of painstaking[4] researches and experiences by the Taekwondo practitioners[5] through their incessant[6] upgrading of technical and spiritual refinement[7]. At the same time, it has been firmly established as a real national martial art enabling the people to defend the nation.

---

1) martial art - n. 군무예, 호전적인 무술
2) proudest - a. proud의 최상급; 자랑할 말한, 훌륭한
3) heritage - n. (대대로) 물려받은 것, 유산; 전통
4) painstaking - a. 수고를 아끼지 않는, 근면한, 성실한
5) practitioner - n. (특히 개업의, 변호사 따위) 개업자
6) incessant - a. 끊임없는, 그칠새 없는
7) refinement - n. 정련, 정제; 세련, 우아; 정밀, 정교

Taekwondo in ancient times

The historical background of Taekwondo development will be explained following the chronological order[8] of 4 different ages; ancient times, middles ages, modern ages and present times.

The origin of Taekwondo

Man by nature has instinct[9] to preserve his own life as well as his race, and therefore engages himself in doing physical activities all the time either consciously or unconsciously.

Man cannot do without physical motions and he grows and developed on them, regardless of time and space. In ancient times people had no means other than the bare hands and body to defend themselves; Even at the times when arms were developed as the defensive[10] or offensive[11] means, people continued to enjoy the bare-hand fighting techniques for the purpose of building physical strength as

---

8) chronological order - n. 연대적인 순서
9) instinct - n. 본능; 직관, 육감, 직감
10) defensive - a. 방어의, 방어용의
11) offensive - a. 공격적인, 공격의

well as showing off through matches at the rituals[12] of tribal communities[13].

In the early history of the Korean peninsula[14], there were three tribes dwelling there, each enjoying warrior's martial art contests during the ritual seasons[15]. At that times people learned techniques from their experiences of fighting against the beasts[16] whose defensive and offensive motions were also the subject of analysis. It is believed that this was exactly the true grounding of today's Taekwondo.

Whose names have descended[17] from "subak", "Taekkyon" and so on. Later in the latter part of ancient times on the Korean peninsula, three kingdoms came into existence always rivaling among them for the hegemony[18]. They were Koguryo, Paekje and Silla all indulged[19] in growing national strength with trained warriors[20]. Therefore, the Korean history tells that there were military personalities among the well-known prominent[21] national

---

12) ritual – a. 의식의; 관습의, 관례의

13) tribal community – n. 부족사회

14) peninsula – n. 반도

15) ritual season – n. 종교적 의식기간

16) beast – n. 짐승, 가축

17) descend – vt. 내리다, 내려가다; (...의) 자손이다, 계통을 잇다

18) hegemony – n. 패권, 주도권, 지배권

19) indulge – vt. (욕망, 정열 따위를) 만족시키다, 충족시키다

20) warrior – n. 전사, 무인; 투사

21) prominent – a. 현저한, 두드러진; 저명한

leaders of the three kingdoms, which proves the military tendency of ruling hierarchy[22].

As a result, youth warrior's corps[23] were organized, such as "hwarando" in Silla and "chouisonin" in Koguryo, which both adopted the martial art training as one of the important subjects of learning. A renowned martial art book of the days, called "muyedobotongji" said "Taekwondo(the art of hand-to-hand fight) is the basis of martial art, enabling one to build strength by means of swing the hand and foot freely and training arms and legs as well as the body to be adaptable to any critical situations, which means Taekwondo was already prevalent in that age.

Thus, it can be easily assumed[24] that Taekwondo was originated from the days of tribal communities on the Korean peninsula. Silla was a kingdom founded in B.C. 57 on the southeastern part of Korea and Koguryo founded in B.C. 37 on the northern part of Korea along the Yalu river, both making great efforts to raise their youngsters into strong warriors called "hwarang" and "sonbae" respectively[25], certainly[26] with Taekwondo as one of the principal subjects of physical training.

---

22) hierarchy - n. (생물) 체계; 성직자 계급; (일반적) 계급제도
23) corps - n. 군단, 병단; 부대
24) assume - vt. 추정하다, 추측(가정)하다
25) respectively - ad. 각각, 각기, 따로따로
26) certainly - ad. 확실히, 꼭; 의심없이

Koguryo's "sonbae" and Taekkyon

Koguryo was founded on the northern part of Korea, surrounded by the hostile[27] han(Chinese) tribes in the north.

Therefore, in its initial stage of national foundation, the kingdom organized a strong warrior's corps called "sonbae" in its attempt to consolidate[28] the centralized power. According to the scholars of history, a man of virtue[29] who never recoils[30] from a fighting means the word "sonbae", which is a member of the warrior's corps.

Later[31] a history book on the old Chosun dynasty described the lift[32] of Koguryo days, saying; "people gathered on march 10 every year at a site[33] of ritual, where they enjoyed a sword dance, archery, subak(taekyon) contests and so on", implying that subak(Taekwondo) was one of the popular events for the ritual in the Koguryo days.

It also said "sonbaes lived in groups, learning history and literary arts at home and going out to construct roads and fortresses[34] for the benefits of society, always devoting themselves to the nations. Therefore, it is altogether natural

---

27) hostile - a. 적의 있는; 적개심이 있는
28) consolidate - vt. 결합하다; 굳게하다, 강화하다
29) virtue - n. 미덕, 덕, 덕행, 선행
30) recoil - vi. 퇴각(패주)하다, 뒷걸음질 치다; 주춤하다
31) later - ad. 뒤에, 나중에
32) lift - n. 상승; 정신의 앙양(고양); (감정의) 고조, 활력 있는 힘
33) site - n. 위치, 장소
34) fortress - n. 요새, 성채; (일반적으로) 안전하고 견고한 곳

that Koguryo put the priority[35] of interests on the Taekkyon which was the basis of martial arts, as can be proved by the wall paintings discovered at several tombs[36] of Koguryo days.

A mural painting[37] at the samsil tomb shows two warriors engaged in a face-to-face match in takkyon(Taekwondo) stance, and a third at the same tomb shows the scene of Korean wrestling bout[38], clearly distinguishing[39] it from the Taekkyon.

It can be assumed from the painting of Taekkyon match that the dead were either a Taekkyon practical or the subject of condolence[40] with dances and martial art.

Silla's "hwarang" and Taekkyon

The kingdom of Silla was founded on the southeastern part of the Korean peninsula under the circumstances[41] of no immediate[42] threat[43] from outside, but along with the

---

35) priority - n. (시간, 순서가) 앞(먼저)임
36) tomb - n. 무덤, 묘
37) mural painting - n. 벽화
38) bout - n. 한판 승부, (권투 따위의) 시합
39) distinguish - vt. 구별하다, 분별(식별)하다
40) condolence - n. 애도, 조상, 조사
41) circumstance - n. 상황, 환경
42) immediate - a. (공간적) 직접의, 바로 이웃의; (시간적) 곧 일어나는, 즉석의
43) threat - n. 위협, 협박

birth of Paekje kingdom on its west flank[44] and the start of invasions[45] by Koguryo from the north, Silla was impelled[46] to arm itself with development of martial arts. In fact, "hwarangdo" is the typical example of Silla's martial arts, which is an assimilation[47] of Koguryo's "sonbae" systems. The members of the youth group of hwarando were well trained with the senses of filial piety[48], loyalty to the kingdom and sacrificial devotion[49] to society to become important personalities for the rein of kingdom. Notable among them were Kim Yu-sin and Kim Chun-chu that made a definite contribution to the unification[50] of those three kingdoms. The chronicle of old Chosun described the life of hwarangs, members of hwarangdo:

"hwarang were selected by the kingdom through contests and, after selection, they lived together in a group, indulging themselves in learning, exercising subak(old form of Taekwondo),

fencing and horse-riding, and sometimes they enjoyed various games of communities, working on emergency

---

44) flank - n. 옆구리, 옆구리 살; 측면
45) invasion - n. 침입, 침략
46) impel - vt. 재촉하다, 몰아대다; 강제로(하여...하게) 하다
47) assimilation - n. 동화
48) filial piety - n. 효심; 충성심
49) sacrificial devotion - n. 희생적인 헌신
50) unification - n. 통일, 단일화, 통합

aids[51] and construction[52] of fortresses and roads, and they were always ready to sacrifice their lives at the time of war."

Hwarangs were particularly influenced by the Buddhistic disciplines[53] and therefore the bronze statues[54] of a warrior(a man of great physical strength) currently exhibited at the kyongju museum[55] clearly indicates that martial art were practiced at temples by showing a strong man's bare-hand defensive and offensive stances.

Especially the shape of a fist[56] shown on the statue of kumgang yoksa(diamond warrior: a strong man) exactly resembles[57] that of a "jungkwon"(right fist) in the contemporary term[58] of Taekwondo.

The statue also shows today's "pyon jumok" (flat fist) and the use of leg, which are seen in today's Taekwondo.

It is really noticeable[59] that in that Silla epoch[60] the terms of "subak"(hand techniques) and "taekkyon" appear together, signifying that both hand foot techniques were used in martial arts as shown in today's Taekwondo.

---

51) emergency aids – n. 비상구조
52) construction – n. 건설, 건축, 구성
53) the Buddhistic disciplines – n. 불교도의 제자들
54) the bronze statues – n. 청동상
55) museum – n. 박물관, 미술관: 기념관
56) fist – n. 주먹, 철권
57) resemble – vt. ...와 공통점이 있다, ...와 닮다
58) contemporary term – n. 동시대의 기간
59) noticeable – a. 눈에 띄는, 이목을 끄는; 두드러진, 현저한
60) epoch – n. (중요한 사건이 일어났던) 시대

Taekwondo transmitted from koguryo to Silla

As the art of Taekwondo was popularized in Koguryo, it was also handed down to Silla, which is justified by the following points of view;

1) "hwarang" (or sonrang) in Silla has the same meaning with the word "sonbae" in Koguryo by indicating both the youth warrior's corps from their etymological origins[61].

2) Both hwarang and sonbae had the same organizations and hierarchical structure with each other.

3) According to historical, as sonbaes in Koguryo used to compete[62] in Taekkyon games at the time of their national festivals, hwarangs in Silla also played Taekkyon games(subak, dokkyonl of Taekkyoni) at such festivals as "palkwanhoe" and "hankawi", thus systematically[63] developing the ancient fighting techniques into the Taekkyon(or sonbae) as the basis of martial arts by around A.D.200.

From the 4th century the hwarangs took the takkyon lesson as a systemized[64] martial art at their learning houses to make it also popularized among ordinary people so much so that their techniques were depicted[65] on the mural

---

61) etymological origins - n. 어원학의 기원
62) compete - vi. 겨루다, 경쟁하다; 서로 맞서다
63) systematically - ad. 체계(조직, 계통)적으로
64) systemize - vt. 조직화하다, 체계화하다
65) depict - vt. (그림, 조각으로) 그리다; (말로) 묘사(서술)하다

paintings of ancient warrior tombs. Again, it is also true that Taekkyon, coming down to Silla, was further developed into a school of martial art with the division of techniques, I, e. bare-hand techniques and foot techniques, which can be proved by the fact that both hand and foot techniques are clearly shown in the ancient sculptures of buddhistic statues.

Taekwondo in the middle age

The Koryo dynasty, which reunified[66] the Korean peninsula after Silla and lasted from A.D. 918 to 1392, had the Teakkyon developed more systematically and made it a compulsory[67] subject in the examinations for selection of military cadets[68]. The techniques and power of Taekkyon martial art grew to become effective weapons even to kill human beings. In the military, a pattern of collective practice, called "obyong-subak-hui(5 soldier's Taekkyon play),

---

66) reunify – vt. 다시 통일(통합)시키다
67) compulsory – a. 강제된, 강제적인; 의무적인, 필수의
68) cadet – n. (미국) 사관학교 생도

was introduced so that it might be used in a real war.

In the early days of Koryo dynasty, martial art abilities were the only required qualifications[69] to become military personnel because the kingdom utterly[70] needed the national defense capabilities[71] after conquer[72] of the peninsula. A certain plan soldier who mastered the Taekkyon techniques was promoted to a general, young were invited to Taekkyon contests and the skilled ones were selected to become military officer. There were lots of other examples in which many Taekkyon-mastered youths were picked up in contests, which is proof that Teakwondo sport was originated in that epoch. The chronicles of Koryo dynasty said; "at a power contest of Taekkyon techniques, lee yi-min punched a pillar of the house with his right-hand fist, then some of the props[73] of the roof were shaken[74]. Another Taekkyon master had his fist pierce[75] through the clay-wall."

Especially the kings of Koryo dynasty were much interested in "subakhui" (Taekkyon contest), making it a

---

69) qualification - n. 자격, 권한
70) utterly - ad. 아주, 전혀, 완전히
71) capability - n. 할 수 있음, 가능성; 능력, 역량,
72) conquer - vt. 정복하다, 공략하다; ...을 이겨내다
73) prop - n. 지주, 버팀목, 버팀대
74) shaken - shake의 과거분사; 흔들다, 뒤흔들다
75) pierce - vt. 꿰찌르다, 꿰뚫다, 관통하다

compulsory course of military training. Therefore, subakhui was also popular out for inspection tours in the villages.

However, the Koryo dynasty in its latest years had gunpower and new types of weapons available at hand, thus slowing down its support of martial arts as the folk games to be transmitted as such down to the modern Korea, Chosun.

Taekwondo in modern times

In the modern times of Korea, which cover the Chosun(or Yi) dynasty (1392-1910), the imperial[76] Korea and the Japanese colonial rule until 1945, Taekwondo was rather called "subakhui" than "Taekkyon" and it suffered an eventual loss of official support from the central government as the weapons were modernized for national defense, although the subakhui was still popular in the early days of Chosun. The Yi dynast(Chosun) was founded on the ideology[77] of Confucianism[78], which resulted in resulted in

76) imperial - a. 황제의; 제국의
77) ideology - n. 관념학, 사회학의 이데올로기
78) Confucianism - n. 공자주의

rejecting all Buddhist festivals and giving more importance on literary art than martial art.

Nonetheless, the annals[79] of Chosun dynasty tell stories about the contests of subakhui ordered by local officials for the purpose of selecting soldiers and others ordered by the kings who enjoyed watching subakhui contests at the times of feasts.

It was also ruled by the defense department that a soldier should be employed when he won out three other contestants in the subakhui bouts. However, as the systematic organization of government progressed, the government officials began to lay more importance on power struggles[80] than on the interest of defense, naturally neglecting promotion of martial arts. Then, it was only in the days of King Jungjo after the disgraceful[81] invasion of Korea by the Japanese (in 1592) that the royal government revived strong defense measures by strengthening military training and martial art practice.

Around this period there was a publication of the so-called muyedobotongji, a book of martial art illustrations, whose 4th volume[82] entitled "hand-fighting techniques"

---

79) annal - n. 연대기, 연대표
80) struggle - vi. 노력하다, 고투하다
81) disgraceful - a. 면목없는, 수치스러운, 불명예스러운
82) volume - n. 책, 서적; 부피, 용적; 양, 분량

contained the illustration of 38 motions, exactly resembling today's Taekwondo Poomsae and basic movements. Of course, those motions cannot be compared with today's Taekwondo Poomsae, which has been modernized through scientific studies.

Even under the Japanese colonial rule, some famous Korean writers, such as Shin Chae-ho and Choi Nam-sun, mentioned about Taekwondo, saying "present subak prevailing[83] in Seoul came from the sonbae in the Koguryo dynasty," and "subak is like today's takkyon which was originally practiced as martial art but is now played mostly by children as game." However, the Japanese colonial government totally prohibited all folkloric[84] games including takkyon in the process of suppressing[85] the Korean people.

The martial art Taekkyondo(Taekwondo) had been secretly handed down only by the masters of the art until the liberation of the country in 1945. Song Duk-ki, one of the then masters, is still alive with the age of over 80 and testifies that his master was Im Ho who was reputed[86] for his excellent skills of Taekkyondo, "jumping over the walls and running through the wood just like a tiger."

---

83) prevail - vi. 널리 보급되다, 유행하다; 우세하다, 극복하다
84) folkloric - a. 민속의
85) suppress - vt. 억압하다, (반란 등을) 진압하다, 가라앉히다
86) repute - vt. 여기다, 생각하다; 평판하다

At that time 14 terms of techniques were used, representing 5 kicking patterns, 4 hand techniques, 3 pushing-down-the-heel patterns, one(1) turning-over kick pattern and 1 technique of downing-the-whole-body.

Also noteworthy[87] is the use the term "poom" which signified a face-to-face stance preparing for a fight. The masters of Taekkyondo were also under constant threat of imprisonment[88], which resulted in an eventual of Taekkyondo as popular games.

Present-day Taekwondo

Upon liberation of Korea from the Japanese colonial rule after world war Ⅱ, the Korean people began recovering the thought of self-reliance[89] and the traditional folkloric games which resumed their popularity. Song Duk-ki, afore-mentioned[90] master of Taekwondo, presented a

---

87) noteworthy - a. 주목할 만한, 현저한
88) imprisonment - n. 투옥, 감금, 구속
89) self-reliance - n. 자기신뢰
90) afore-mentioned - 앞에서 언급한 바와 같이

demonstration[91] of the martial art before the first Republic of Korea President Syngman Rhee on the occasion of the latter's birthday anniversary, thus clearly distinguishing Taekwondo from the Japanese karate which had been introduced by the Japanese rulers.

Martial art exports began opening their Taekwondo gymnasia all over the country and after the end of Korean war(1950-1953) Taekwondo was popularized among the dan-grade black-belters within the country, also dispatching about 2,000 Taekwondo masters to more than 100 countries for foreigner's training.

After all, following the nomination of Taekwondo as a national martial art in 1971, the present Kukkiwon was founded in 1972 to be used as the central gymnasium as well as the site of various Taekwondo competitions[92]. Then a year later on May 28, 1973 the World Taekwondo Championships was organized, the final results of which up to 1985.

Again in 1974, Taekwondo was admitted[93] to the Asian games as an official event. In 1975 Taekwondo was accepted as an official sport by the U.S Amateur Athletic

---

91) demonstration - n. 증명; 논증; 증거
92) competition - n. 경쟁, 겨루기; 경기, 시합
93) admit - vt. (입회, 입학, 입국)을 허가하다

Union(AAU) and also admitted to the General Association[94] of International Sports Federations[95](GAISF), followed by the adoption of official sports event by the international council of military sports(CISM) in 1976. In 1979, president of the World Taekwondo Federation(WTF) was elected President of the world federation of non-Olympic sports. The WTF became an IOC-recognized sports federation in 1980, making Taekwondo an Olympic sport. Then the adoption of Taekwondo as an official event was followed by the World Games in 1981, the Pan-American games in 1986, and finally by the 2000 Olympiad held in Australia.

* 참고 : The above contents trace a quotation to its original source from internet in kukkiwon web sight

---

94) association - n. 연합; 협회, 조합, 회
95) federation - n. 동맹, 연합, 연맹

CHAPTER 3

Eight instructive stories

The life of Isaac Newton

It was on Christmas Day when Isaac Newton was born in 1642. He grew up in the English countryside. From childhood Newton was very interested in the mysteries[1] of nature. The question of motion was one of the most difficult scientific problems in Newton's day. Why did objects move? Scientists wanted to find out the reason why stones rolled down hills, why wind blew leaves along the ground, and why heavy objects fell to the earth when dropped. After Copernicus, they began to admit that the earth itself moved. They came to believe that there must be laws that govern these various kinds of motion. The Greeks believed there were different rules for motion on earth and in space, and that there were unnatural movements on the earth.

Galileo, an Italian scientist, was the first person to challenge this Greek view of motion. He was a follower of Copernicus[2]. It didn't make much sense to Galileo[3] to have different rules for motion on earth and in space.

Two important discoveries were made by him. First, he

---

1) mystery – n. 신비, 불가사의, 비밀
2) Copernicus – n. 코페르니쿠스(지동설을 제창한 폴란드의 천문학자)
3) Galileo – n. 갈릴레오(이태리의 천문학자, 물리학자)

showed that motion was not unnatural. On the contrary[4], an object once in motion would continue in motion. Second, he worked out a mathematical formula[5] for the motion of all objects that fell to the earth. But Galileo was not able to explain how all motion in the universe worked. Much work had been done since Copernicus to record the movements of the solar system. It remained now for some great mathematical mind to pull this work all together and put it into universal laws.

When Newton was twenty-three, he moved from Cambridge to his country home. There his thoughts turned to the problems of motion. One evening Isaac Newton was sitting in the garden. He fell into a deep thought, when he happened to notice a falling apple. The apple set him to wondering about the movement of falling things.

It occurred to him that the force which caused fruit to fall from trees worked quite as well at greater distances from the center of the earth-on top of buildings or even on top of mountains. Perhaps, thought Newton, this same force still reached out much farther, even to the moon. Was it this force which kept the moon going around the earth?

And if so, couldn't the same force explain the movements

---

4) on the contrary - 이에 반하여, 도리어, ...은 커녕
5) mathematical formula - 수학적인 공식

of the planets[6] around the sun? Newton began to search for a mathematical expression of his idea. In 1669 Newton became professor of mathematics at Cambridge. A few years later he began to study the problems of motion again. He had already discovered the essential ideas, but it still remained for him to solve the difficult mathematical problems. At last he seemed to have solved the main difficulties. But he did not publish his findings at once. Only in 1687 did he at last publish his new work. Newton's great work, The Mathematical Principles of Natural Philosophy[7], marked the triumph[8] of the Scientific Revolution. The very title is important. Newton had found the mathematical principles, the scientific laws which governed the movements of the earth and the heavens. The book completed the working out of a new view of nature, a task begun by Copernicus. The result was an exact mathematical world. Three laws of motion were put forward in the book. The first law stated that bodies will move in a straight line with uniform motion unless acted upon by a force. Thus, a bullet shot from a gun moves straight ahead until it is stopped by a target or it slows and falls as a result of the friction[9] caused by moving through air.

---

6) planet - n. (천문학) 행성; 지구; 천체(태양, 달 등)

7) The mathematical principles of natural philosophy - 순수철학의 수학적인 원리

8) triumph - n. 승리; 대성공, 개가, 업적

9) friction - n. (두 물체의) 마찰; 알력, 불화

The second law stated that the acceleration of a body is in proportion[10] to the force applied to the body. Thus, the harder you throw a ball, the faster it will move. The third law said that every action has an equal and opposite reaction[11]. Thus, when you hit a punching bag, it comes right back at you. Newton also worked out a mathematical expression for gravity[12]. It applied equally to the apple falling from the tree and the moon going around the earth. Newton was soon recognized as the leader of English science. Science was never quite the same after Newton's discoveries. Little wonder that an eighteenth-century poet, Alexander Pope, looking back at Newton's work, wrote: "Nature and Nature's laws lay hid in night; God said, Let Newton be!-And all was light."

Newton, however, never rested on his fame[13]. He continued to work and study. In his last years he once said to a friend, "I do not know what I may appear to the world, but to myself I seem to have been only like a boy, playing on the seashore, and then finding a smooth pebble[14] or a pretty shell, while the great ocean of truth lay undiscovered before me."

---

10) proportion - n. 비, 비율; 조화, 균형; 부분, 몫, 할당
11) reaction - n. 반응, 반작용, 반동
12) gravity - n. (물리) 중력, 지구인력; 중량, 무게
13) fame - n. 명성, 명예; 평판, 풍문
14) pebble - n. 조약돌, 자갈

The Green Frog

Once upon a time, there lived a green frog[15] who would never do what his mother told him. If she told him to go east, he would go west. If she asked him to go up the mountain, he would run down to the river. Never, never would the green frog obey his mother for the world. His mother grew very old, still worrying[16] about her son's future. At last she fell ill and realized that she was about to die. So she called her son to her beside and said to him, "My dear son, I shall not live any longer. When I die, do not bury[17] me on the mountain. Do you hear? I want to be buried by the river." She meant of course that she wanted to be buried on the mountain, for she well knew of her son's perverse[18] ways. Very soon afterwards she died. Then the green frog was very sad and wept long. He repented of all his misdeeds[19] in the past and made up his mind that now at least he would do as his mother had asked. So he buried her by the riverside. Whenever it

---

15) frog - n. 개구리
16) worry - vi. 걱정(근심)하다, 고민하다
17) bury - vt. 묻다, (흙 따위로) 덮다;...을 장례하다, 매장하다
18) perverse - a. 외고집의, 심술궂은, 성미가 비꼬인
19) misdeed - n. 악행, 비행, 범죄

rained, he worried lest her grave should be washed away. He used to sit and weep in a sad voice. And that's why the green frog croaks whenever it is likely to rain.

The poisonous persimmons[20]

A Buddhist priest[21] once kept a big store of dried persimmons in a cupboard in his room. He planned to eat them all himself, and so he told his young disciple[22], "These are deadly poison. If you take even the smallest bit of it, you will die within an hour. See that you leave them as they are." But one day the young disciple ate all the persimmons in the cupboard. Then he broke the holder of his master's inkstone[23], which his master had been most highly prizing. Finally he went to lie on his bed, covering himself with blankets. A little later the priest returned. When he saw his disciple, he cried, "Whatever is the matter with you?" His disciple answered, "Through my carelessness I dropped the holder of your inkstone and broke it. I realized that was an unpardonable crime[24]. The only thing left for me to do was to put an end to my life, and so I went to your cupboard and

---

20) poisonous persimmon - 독이 든 감
21) Buddhist priest - 불교의 성직자
22) disciple - n. 제자, 문하생
23) inkstone - n. 벼루
24) unpardonable crime - a. 용서할 수 없는 죄

ate all the poison you had kept there. Now I lie here waiting to breathe my last." The priest was so tickled[25] by his disciple's ingenuity[26] that he could not help laughing and said no more about the matter.

The ungrateful tiger

One day a tiger was trapped[27] in a pit[28]. It asked a passing traveler to rescue[29] it, promising to reward him. The traveler reached a long branch down into the pit, and the tiger could come out of it. But when it was safe again, it turned on the traveler and roared with its mouth wide open, "I am very hungry and I am going to eat you up." The traveler scolded[30] the tiger. " You are most ungrateful[31]," he said, "How can you eat me when I have saved you? But the tiger ignored his words and so the traveler appealed to a toad which lived under a nearby rock. The traveler told the toad of the beast's ingratitude[32], but the tiger insisted that it was hungry and mean to eat the

---

25) tickle - vt. 기쁘게 하다, 즐겁게 하다, 만족시키다

26) ingenuity - n. 발명의 재주, 현명함, 재주

27) trap - n. 올가미, 덫; vt. ...을 덫으로 잡다, 덫을 놓다

28) pit - n. 구덩이, 구멍

29) rescue - vt. 구조하다, 구하다

30) scold - vt. 꾸짖다, ...에게 잔소리하다

31) ungrateful - a. 은혜를 모르는, 감사할 줄 모르는

32) ingratitude - n. 배은망덕, 은혜를 모름

traveler. "I must look into this more closely," said the toad. "Will you show me the place where it happened?" So they went along to the pit. Then the toad asked the tiger, "How did it happen? Let me see just where you were." So the tiger jumped down into the pit and said, "I was down here at the bottom, see." But the traveler took the branch out of the pit and said, "Of course, this wasn't there then." The toad turned to the traveler and said with a smile, "You had better go now, and from now on don't help such ungrateful creatures."

Looking down at the tiger in the pit it said, "You ungrateful wretch[33]! You can stay down there now." The traveler thanked the toad[34] and went on his way. The tiger trapped in the pit roared[35] in a fury[36], but the toad went back to its home under the rock and refused to help it.

---

33) wretch - n. 가엾은 사람, 비참한 사람
34) toad - n. 두꺼비; 징그러운 놈, 경멸할 인물, 어리석은 녀석
35) roar - vi. (짐승 따위가) 으르렁대다, 포효하다
36) fury - n. 격노, 격분

Antony and Cleopatra

Cleopatra, Queen of Egypt, was known throughout the ancient world for her beauty and intelligence. It was said that any man who met her would fall in love with her.

Antony, who ruled Rome with two others after the death of Julius Caesar, went to the East to meet Cleopatra and discover whether she was plotting[37] against Rome. When he first saw Cleopatra, she was floating down a river on a splendid sailing ship made of gold. The oars were made of silver and moved in time to music. The sails were purple[38] and gave out a sweet scent. Cleopatra lay on this ship and by her side were boys with fans to keep her cool. Antony was overcome by this sight and, like many men before him, he fell in love with Cleopatra when they met face to face.

She also fell in love with Antony, who was as famous for his success in war and his political power as Cleopatra was for her beauty. She wanted him to live in Egypt for ever. Antony stayed in Egypt enjoying the lazy[39] and luxurious[40] life to which Cleopatra and her friends were accustomed[41].

---

37) plot - n. 음모; (비밀) 계획; 책략
38) purple - a. 자줏빛의, 진홍색, 새빨간 n. 자줏빛
39) lazy - a. 게으른, 나태한, 게으름장이의
40) luxurious - a. 호화스러운, 사치스러운
41) accustom - vt. 익숙케 하다, 습관이 들게 하다

He tried to forget what was happening in Rome and his real purpose in coming to the East. Then news came from Rome that Antony's wife had died. Antony was needed at home to help fight the enemies who were moving closer to Rome. He decided that he must leave Egypt, and sadly said good-bye to Cleopatra.

Antony's fellow rulers in Rome, Octavius and Lepidus, had been growing angry at Antony's life of pleasure in Egypt. Octavius complained[42] that he was drinking and eating and wasting his time in merry-making while Rome's great enemy, Pompey, was bringing his army closer. When Antony arrived in Rome he found that his friendship with these two had cooled. He felt that he had to do something to regain[43] the respect of his friends, particularly Octavius who was known to be ambitious and eager[44] to rule Rome alone. And so it was decided that Antony would marry Octavia, the sister of Octavius.

She was beautiful, gentle, and modest and in character quite unlike Cleopatra who was too proud. In fact, if Antony had not loved Cleopatra he would have considered Octavia a perfect wife. The wedding was arranged for political reasons and regained the friendship between

---

42) complain - vi. 불평하다, 한탄하다 vt. ...라고 불평하다
43) regain - vt. 회복하다, 다시 찾다
44) eager - a. 열망하는, 간절히 바라는

Antony and Octavius. Cleopatra was so angry that she wanted to kill the messenger who brought the news. However, when she had calmed down, she asked the messenger questions about Octavia's appearance and character. He replied that Octavius was plain, short, old, poor in speech and crept rather than walked. Delighted at this reply, and content that Octavia was not her rival for Antony's love, Cleopatra rewarded the messenger with gold. Although Antony treated his new wife with great kindness and respect, he longed to be back in Egypt with Cleopatra. A fortune-teller[45] told him that Octavius would become more powerful than he, and that he should return to Egypt where he could forget his worries about Octavius' ambition[46]. He decided to take the fortune-teller's advice but before he could make preparations to leave Rome, Antony was called to a meeting. He was required to attend, with Octavius and Lepidus, a meeting in which they would try to persuade[47] Pompey to agree to peace terms.

---

45) fortune-teller - n. 예언을 말하는 사람
46) ambition - n. 대망, 야망, 야심
47) persuade - vt. 설득하다, 권유(재촉, 독촉)하여...시키다

It was agreed that Pompey would receive Sicily and Sardinia. In return he agreed to rid the sea of pirates[48]. Both sides would return their prisoners of war. The peace agreement was celebrated with a feast at which Lepidus behaved foolishly and became drunk. It was clear that he was the weakest of the three rulers of Rome.

After the peace agreement, Antony and Octavia left Rome for Athens. Octavius seemed very unhappy to see them go. In Athens, however, news came that Octavius had gone to war again with Pompey. Moreover, he had dishonored[49] Antony's reputation[50], in spite of the fact that he was now his brother-in-law. Antony sent Octavia back to Rome to talk to her brother, with the message that he would go to war against Octavius if he did not stop spreading bad rumours about him. Octavia arrived in Rome and was greeted by her brother with the news that Antony had gone back to Cleopatra and was preparing war against him. He persuaded Octavia that she had been badly treated by Antony and should remain in Rome. Even the fact of Antony's marriage to his sister did not prevent[51] Octavius from wanting to destroy Antony. He wanted to be the only

---

48) pirate - n. 해적; 해적선 vt. 약탈하다
49) dishonor - n. 명예; 치욕, 굴욕 vt. ...에게 굴욕을 주다; ...의 이름을 더럽히다
50) reputation - n. 평판, 명성
51) prevent - vt. 막다, 방해하다, 막아서...못하게 하다

ruler of Rome. Lepidus was weak and could easily be got out of power but a war against Antony was necessary.

Antony had gathered his army at Actium and was joined there by Cleopatra. News came that Octavius was approaching Actium with his navy. Antony's advisers told him that he must fight on land because his ships were old and had not been used for a long time and his sailors were inexperienced[52] whereas Octavius had a new and efficient navy. Antony's soldiers, who had had many military successes, could certainly beat[53] he enemy's army on land. Antony, however, did not listen to this good advice and preferred to be persuaded by Cleopatra, who wanted him to fight a sea battle. Antony's navy was defeated and his ships were sunk[54]. Cleopatra was partly to blame for this. When she had seen that the battle was going badly, she had commanded her navy to sail back to Egypt. Antony, having lost everything, told his followers to escape and followed Cleopatra to Egypt. Antony recovered his courage when he saw how dishonorably[55] Octavius treated him. He sent a message to Octavius, who by this time had arrived in Egypt with his army, challenging him to a fight, man to man.

---

52) inexperience - n. 미경험, 미숙련, 미숙, 서투름
53) beat - vt. 치다, 두드리다; 때려 부수다
54) sunk - sink의 과거, 과거분사; 가라앉다, 침몰하다
55) dishonorably - ad. 불명예스러운

Octavius refused to fight in that way, saying "Let the old fool know that I have many other ways to die." A battle could not be avoided.

Octavius was confident[56] that his forces were superior to Antony's and besides, he now had in his army many of Antony's followers. Antony, feeling sure that he was going to die, said good-bye to Cleopatra and led his army against the forces of Octavius. To everyone's surprise, Antony's army won the battle. With all his confidence regained, Antony prepared for another battle to finally drive Octavius out of Egypt. But the second battle was fought at sea and, as before, Antony lost. All his followers had gone over to the other side. Antony realized he had lost everything and in despair[57] he accused Cleopatra, "You have betrayed[58] me, false soul of Egypt. My love for you has led to my shame and defeat." His anger made him mad and he wanted to kill Cleopatra. "This witch shall die, for she has sold me to the young Roman boy!"

Cleopatra escaped from him in terror. She hid herself and sent a messenger to tell Antony that she had died. Antony, left alone, decided that the only honorable thing left for him to do was to kill himself. But he was afraid.

---

56) confident - a. 확신하는, 자신이 있는
57) despair - n. 절망; 자포자기
58) betray - vt. 배반하다; 속이다; 누설하다

"I, who once ruled a quarter of the world with my sword, now have even less courage than a women.

What Cleopatra has done, I must ask someone else to do for me." He begged his faithful servant to kill me, but the servant, instead of taking Antony's life, killed himself. Seeing that even his servant had more courage than he, Antony fell on his sword. The sword only wounded him and he was too weak to finish it properly[59]. He begged passer-by to put him out of his misery[60], but they all refused to kill him. Then, Cleopatra, realizing what Antony would do, sent a messenger, too late, to tell him that she was still alive.

Antony was carried, dying, to where Cleopatra was hiding. He was comforted[61] by Cleopatra in his last moments, and when he died, Cleopatra was speechless with grief. Octavius promised Cleopatra that he would treat her well, but warned her that if she, too, took her own life he would not be so kind to her heir. But Cleopatra decided that she could not go on living without Antony. She told her servants to bring her crown[62] and her robes[63] of state[64].

---

59) properly – ad. 당연히, 정당하게; 올바르게, 정확히
60) misery – n. 불행, (정신적) 고통
61) comfort – n. 위로, 위안
62) crown – n. 왕관
63) robe – n. 관복, 예복
64) state – n. 국가, 나라; 국토; 정부

And so, dressed like a queen, she prepared for death. On her throat and her arm she placed two snakes whose bites[65] were deadly poisonous and killed a person instantly and painlessly. Cleopatra, who in her life had been guilty of so many cowardly acts, died bravely.

Octavius found her and was full of grief at the death of such a great queen. He told her servants to carry her away, "She shall be buried by the side of Antony. No other grave in the world shall contain such a famous pair as this queen and her brave soldier."

Make the most of your life

Eight months ago I left wonju. Sometimes it seems like it was years ago. Sometimes it seems like it was only yesterday. I have seen many different customs and learned many important lessons in life. Last July, my family moved to Perth, Australia. My father is an engineer with a large Korean mining company. He would work in Australia for

---

65) bite - vt. 물다, 물어뜯다

two years. I remember our family talks in wonju. Should the family go with him? Should we remain in Korea while he's away? What are the good points and bad points of going together? We finally decided that this would be a good opportunity for all of us. Our family would go to Australia together!

At that time, it didn't seem real. I didn't know very much about Australia. I knew almost nothing about Perth[66]. Therefore, when I arrived in Australia, it was like a dream.

Sometimes I felt like a tree. I just stood where I was and watched things. That lasted for about a month. I felt sorry for myself.

I missed my friends, Korean food, Korean television programs, and much more. Sometimes I was so lonely that I wanted to cry. But of course, I couldn't cry. I was a tree. Then, I met Fred and everything changed. Fred and I were in two classes together; math and science. In Korea, I was a pretty good student in English. My grades were always high. But in Australian school, I was lost. I could understand only about half of what the teachers said. I felt so confused, except in math class. One day, a rather short boy with red hair and glasses asked me a question. My life as a tree was coming to an end.

---

66) Perth - 호주 남서부의 도시이름

That day after class, red haired Fred asked me why I didn't talk with anyone. It sounds like an easy question, but how could I answer? After all[67], trees don't talk. I told him that my English was not very good, but Fred wouldn't give up. He was a good listener. We sat outside the school and talked with each other for hours. He had many questions for me. Where did I come from? How long would I be in Australia? Did I like sports? Did I like music? Then he asked me if I missed Korea. I explained that I missed my country more than anything in the world. He could see that I was sad.

Fred thought for a moment, then said something I will never forget. Fred said, "Sometimes we can't be where we want to be. Sometimes we can't be with the people we'd like to be with. Sometimes the things we have to do are very difficult and make us feel uncomfortable[68]. But life is a precious[69] gift, and life is very short. We have to make the most of that gift every day, or we waste it."

Since then, Fred and I have become best of friends. From him, I have learned a very important lesson in life. We have to make the most of every situation. If we do, good things happen. This simple truth is understood by all great people

---

67) after all – 결국, 요컨대, 역시; 어쨌든
68) uncomfortable – a. (사람, 물건 따위가) 불유쾌한, 기분이 언짢은
69) precious – a. 비싼, 귀중한, 가치가 있는

and by all happy people, too. Now, I also understand.

Laughing with life

I think laughter must have been the original language of the Garden of Eden. "Laugh, and the world laughs with you; weep[70], and you weep alone." This is one of the best-known English proverbs. It shows us the importance of laughter in society, and helps us improve our understanding of English culture. Some people have a keen sense of humor[71], others do not.

Sense of humor, is part of a person's character. If someone has no sense of humor, we feel that he lacks something very important. He cannot see the funny side of life. He takes everything too seriously.

In other words, he is boring[72]. We are attracted to people who have a sense of humor, who can laugh at the same things we laugh at. Maybe you will like these jokes.

---

70) weep - vi. 눈물을 흘리다, 울다, 비탄하다
71) humor - n. 유머, 해학
72) bore - vt. ...에 구멍을 뚫다, 도려내다

humor 1.

A math teacher said to one of his young students: "Do you know why number 11 is afraid of number 7?" The student said, "No, that sounds like a strange question. Why was 11 afraid?" The teacher replied, "Because seven, ate nine and ten." The student thought for a while, then laughed at the silly[73] riddle[74].

humor 2.

A lady telephoned to her grocer[75] and said, "I sent my son, Tom, to your shop for three pounds of apples. I weighed them, and you didn't give him three pounds. Your scales must be wrong." "My scales are not wrong," said the grocer. "I certainly weighed the apples. But have you weighed Tom?"

humor 3.

A little girl was going to her friend's birthday party. Before she left home, her mother told her to be a good little girl. She should remember to thank her friend's mother for

---

73) silly - a. 어리석은; 분별없는, 바보 같은
74) riddle - n. 수수께끼, 알아맞히기
75) grocer - n. 식료품상인; 식료잡화상

the nice party before she returned home. When the little girl got home, her mother asked her if she had remembered to thank her hostess[76]. The little girl replied, "Oh, no. I heard another little girl thanking her for the nice party, and the hostess replied, Don' t mention it, - so I didn' t."

humor 4.

A farmer who lived in a small village suffered from severe chest pains and loss of memory[77]. The village doctor tried many things, but couldn' t cure[78] him. So the farmer decided that he would visit a doctor in the town. But he was told that a patient had to pay three pounds for the first visit and one pound for the second visit. The miserly farmer thought about this for a long time, and then he decided to go to the doctor in the town. As he came into the doctor' s office, he said, "Nice to see you again, doctor." The doctor asked him a few questions, examined his chest, and then took the pound which the farmer insisted on giving him. Then the doctor said with a smile, "Well, sir. There' s nothing new. Please continue to take the same medicine I gave you the first time you came to see me."

---

76) hostess - n. 여주인
77) loss of memory - n. 기억상실
78) cure - n. 치료, 치료법

humor 5.

A man was laying a new concrete[79] path. While the cement was still wet, he went away to have his lunch. While he was away, a crowd of children ran across the wet cement, leaving their footprints in the hardening[80] surface. When the man returned and saw what the children had done, he began shouting at them for spoiling[81] his morning' s work. A neighbor who heard him shouting at the children said: "I thought you liked children, George." "He replied: "I do like them-in the abstract[82], but not in the concrete."

Improving your study habits

Maybe you are like most students. You may not be satisfied with all of your subjects. You occasionally[83] get good grades in some subjects, but not in others. Have you

---

79) concrete - a. 콘크리트(제)의; 굳어진, 고체의; 구체적으로
80) harden - vt. 딱딱하게 하다, 굳히다
81) spoil - vt. 망쳐놓다, 못쓰게 만들다, 손상하다
82) in the abstract - 추상적으로
83) occasionally - ad. 이따금씩, 때때로

ever thought of the reason for this? Why don't you take this opportunity? Poor grades may be because you are interested in other things. Or it may be that you don't know how to study well.

If you think you can never be a top student, you are mistaken. Good study habits can help you to become a better scholar. If you are interested, you had better remember some important points. Here is a list of useful suggestions.

Plan your time carefully.

Suppose you are planning a trip. The first thing you must do is make a list of things to take. If you don't, you are almost certain to leave something important at home. When you plan your week, you should make a list of things that you have to do. Otherwise[84], you may forget to leave enough time to complete an important task. After making the list, you should make a schedule of your time. Your list ought to include time for eating, sleeping, dressing, being at school, meeting friends, and so on. Then, decide on a good, regular time for studying. Be sure to set aside enough time to complete the work that you normally do each week.

---

84) otherwise - ad. 딴 방법으로, 그렇지는 않고; 만약 그렇지 않으면

Don't forget time for entertainment[85], hobbies, and maybe just relaxation[86]. A weekly schedule may not solve all your problems, but it will help you see what is happening to you.

Finding a good place to study.

Look around the house for a good place. Keep this space free of everything but study materials. Your space may be a desk or simply a corner in your room. No games, radios, or television! If you can't find such a place at home, find a library near your house. When you sit down to work, concentrate[87] on the subject!

Scan before you read.

This means looking a passage over quickly before you read it carefully. Scanning[88] lets you preview[89] the material and get a general idea of the information. This will allow you to skip[90] less important materials when you begin to read. Scanning will help you double your reading speed and

---

85) entertainment - n. 대접, 환대; 연예, 여흥; 연회, 주연, 파티
86) relaxation - n. 완화, 풀림, 이완
87) concentrate - vt. 집중하다. 한 점에 모으다
88) scan - vi. (얼굴 등을) 자세히 쳐다보다, 자세히 조사하다, 세밀히 살피다
89) preview - n. 예비검사; 시연, 시사
90) skip - vi. 가볍게 뛰다, 깡충깡충 뛰다

improve your comprehension.

Make good use of your time in class.

You need good classroom habits. Take advantage of what the teacher says in class. Careful listening in class means less work later. Taking notes will help you remember what the teachers say. When a teacher gets off the subject, stop taking notes.

Study regularly.

When you get home from class, go over your notes. Review the important points made in class. Read any related material in your textbook. Read that material your teacher is going to discuss[91] the next day. This will help you understand the next class better. If you do these things regularly, the material will become more meaningful. You will also remember it longer.

Develop a good attitude[92] about tests.

The purpose of a test is to see what you have learned

---

91) discuss - vt. 토론(논의)하다, ...에 관하여 (서로) 이야기하다
92) attitude - n. (사람, 물건 등에 대한) 태도, 마음가짐

about a subject. Try not to become overly worried. Tests do more than just provide grades. Tests let you know what you need to study more. They also help make your new knowledge last longer.

There are other techniques that might help you to achieve better results in your studies. Only a handful[93] have been mentioned here. You will probably discover many others after you have tried these.

Nature's own doctor

When I was a farm boy, I kept many wild animals as pets. One of my favorite animals was a deer. Unfortunately, the deer's side was once badly cut by a sharp wire fence. I cleaned the wound and put a bandage on it, but the deer pulled the bandage off. Then he carefully licked[94] the hair away from the cut, so that the air and sun could get at it. He himself took care of his trouble and was soon healed[95]. I

---

93) handful – n. 한 움큼, 한 줌, 손에 그득
94) lick – vt. 핥다; (물결이) 스치다, 넘실거리다
95) heal – vt. (병, 상처, 마음 등을) 고치다, 낫게 하다

also used to have a squirrel[96]. I kept it in a big cage[97]. One night she caught her leg in a wire. In trying to get it loose, she broke it. For days she lay with her broken leg in the same position.

Although she had jumped around so much before, she suddenly became quiet. She healed herself by keeping still. The way animals take care of wounds is amazing. A water rat will cover a wound with tree gum to keep out dirt. Bears also cover their wounds with tree gum[98] and sometimes with wet earth. But a water rat will not use earth. He knows that it would wash off if he goes into the water. Monkeys will try to stop bleeding[99] by holding a wound with their hands. Then they will cover it with clean leaves. Some birds seem to know about healing a broken wing. I have seen a wild turkey[100] with a broken wing lie down in a certain position. With his bill, he put his wing together and held it still so that the bones would heal. The break mended completely, though the wing did not have the same sharp as the other one. A woodcock[101] with a

---

96) squirrel - n. 다람쥐
97) cage - n. 새장, 우리
98) gum - n. 고무질, 점성 고무
99) bleeding - n. 출혈, 유혈
100) turkey - n. 칠면조
101) woodcock - n. 조류(누른 도요)

broken leg will put clay around it to hold it in place. Sometimes he will use roots to make it stronger. When a wild creature is hurt, he usually goes away by himself to a quiet place. Then, besides taking care of his wound, he may eat certain plants as medicine. Members of the cat and dog families eat grass when they are not well. Wild bears eat berries[102] and roots. Deer eat tender bark and certain small branches of trees.

An animal with fever always hunts for a cool place, near[103] water. He lies quiet, eats very little, and drinks water often until he is well.

On the other hand, an animal with soreness in his joints and muscles always hunts for the hottest spot he can find in the sunlight.

He gets all the heat possible. With the changing seasons, birds and animals seem to know they need to eat different kinds of food.

Deer[104] will travel miles to drink water that has lime[105] in it.

They need lime to make their horns[106] grow.

---

102) berry - n. 핵없는 식용 소과일(주로 딸기류)
103) near - ad. 가까이, 근접하여 prep. ...에 가까이, ...에 가깝게
104) deer - n. 사슴
105) lime - n. 석회 vt. 석회로 소독하다, ...에 석회를 뿌리다
106) horn - n. 뿔, 사슴뿔

Birds that lay eggs need lime to form eggshells[107]. From far inland, birds will fly to the seashore, where they can find shellfish[108].

They have to have lime, and they know that by eating shellfish they can get it.

Sick or hurt animals often use nature's aids: plant medicines, fresh air, and complete rest.

It is wonderful the way animals and birds heal themselves. As you know, our ancestors[109] learned much from watching the animals.

We still use many ways which were handed down to us.

In this sense, man, plant, and animal live together, each helping the others. It is in this fact that the wisdom of nature is revealed!

* 참고 : The adove contents trace a quotation to its original source from high school English for everyone.

---

107) eggshell - n. 달걀 껍데기
108) shellfish - n. 조개, 갑각류(새우, 게 따위)
109) ancestor - n. 선조, 조상

William Tell

The people of Switzerland were not always free and happy as they are today. Many years ago a proud tyrant whose name was Gessler, ruled over them, and made their lot a bitter[110] one indeed. One day this tyrants set up a tall pole in the public square[111], and put his own cap on the top of it; and then he gave orders that every man who came into the town should bow down before it. But there was one man, named William Tell, who would not do this. He stood up straight with folded[112] arms, and laughed at the swinging cap. He would not bow down to Gessler himself. When Gessler heard of this, he was very angry. He was afraid that other men would disobey, and that soon the whole country would rebel[113] against him. So he made up his mind to punish the bold[114] man. William Tell's home was among the mountains, and he was a famous hunter. No one in all the land could shoot with bow and arrow so well as he. Gessler knew this, and so he thought of cruel plan to make the hunter's own skill bring him to grief. He ordered that

---

110) bitter - a. 쓴, 모진, 살을 에는 (듯한)
111) in the public square - 시민광장
112) fold - vt. (팔 따위를) 끼다, 감다
113) rebel - vt. 모반하다, 배반하다; 반항하다
114) bold - a. 대담한, 담찬, 담력이 있는

Tell's little boy should be made to stand up in the public square with an apple on his head; and then he bade Tell shoot the apple with one of his arrows.

Tell begged[115] the tyrant not to have him make this test of his skill. What if the boy should move? What if the bowman's hand should tremble[116]? What if the arrow should not carry true? "Will you make me kill my boy?" he said. "Say no more." said Gessler. "You must hit the apple with your one arrow. If you fail, my soldiers shall kill the boy before your eyes." Then, without another word, Tell fitted[117] the arrow to his bow. He took aim, and let it fly. The boy stood firm and still. He was not afraid, for he had all faith in his father's skill. The arrow whistled[118] through the air. It struck[119] the apple fairly in the center, and carried it away. The people who saw it shouted with joy. As Tell was turning away from the place, an arrow which he had hidden under his coat dropped to the ground. "Fellow!" cried Gessier, "what mean you with this second arrow?" "Tyrant[120]!" was Tell's proud answer, "this arrow was for your heart if I had hurt my child." And there is an old story

---

115) beg - vt. (먹고 입을 것, 돈, 허가, 은혜 따위를) 빌다, 구하다
116) tremble - vi. 떨다, 전율하다, 와들와들 떨다
117) fit - a. (꼭) 맞는, 알맞은, 적당한
118) whistle - n. 휘파람; vi. 휘파람소리를 내다, ...을 울리다
119) struck - strike의 과거, 과거분사; vt. 치다, 때리다; (타격을) 가하다, 타격하다
120) tyrant - n. 폭군, 압제자

that, not long after this, Tell did shoot the tyrant with one of his arrows; and thus he set his country free.

CHAPTER 4
Athletics

Golf

The game of golf undoubtedly grew from field hockey, the forerunner[1] of all stick and ball games. Many authorities believe a golf type of game was played today, originated in Scotland in the 14th century. Scottish Parliamentary[2] action forbidding the game as a threat to the development of skill at archery, and thus of national defense, deterred[3] the game only briefly until King James Ⅳ became a fan and golf was played openly.

Unlike many sports, golf has been a woman's game for centuries. Mary Queen of Scots was an enthusiastic[4] and skilled golfer. Her attentive army cadet was the forerunner of the caddy[5] of today. Appropriately[6] the most famous course in the world is the Royal and Ancient Golf Club of St. Andrews, Scotland, founded in 1754. It remains the seat of authority for all matters pertaining[7] to Canada and the United States in the latter part of the 19th century. John G.

---

1) forerunner - n. 선구자, 선인; 선조
2) Scottish parliamentary - 스코틀랜드 의회
3) deter - vt. (공포, 의혹 따위로) 제지하다, 단념시키다; 방해하다, 저지하다
4) enthusiastic - a. 열심의; 열광적인; 열성적인, 열렬한
5) caddy - n. (골프) 캐디; 심부름꾼
6) appropriately - ad. 적당히, 상당하게
7) pertain - vi. 속하다, 부속하다; 관계하다; 적합하다, 어울리다

Reid introduced the game to his friends in a cow pasture[8] in Yonkers, New York, in 1885. This Scotsman, who became known as the "Father of American Golf," was instrumental in establishing the first golf club, St. Andrews of Yonkers, in 1888.

Five of the private clubs in the Eastern United States joined together to form the United States Golf Association in 1984. From its beginning, the U.S.G.A[9] has been the ruling body for amateurs and the sponsoring body for prominent[10] tournaments.

Early in the 20th century enthusiastic women golfers were granted playing privileges[11] at private courses and numerous public and college courses were built. The development of equipment for consistent[12] and accurate play and mass manufacturing brought the price of golf within the range of millions.

Today golf continues to attract many new followers. Men and women professional teachers encourage all ages to participate through their clinic[13], individual teaching, and examples of excellent play. At present more than 6500

---

8) pasture - n. 목장, 방목장; 목초지
9) U.S.G.A - United States Golf Association의 약자(미국골프협회)
10) prominent - a. 현저한, 두드러진; 저명한, 걸출한
11) privilege - n. 특권; 특전; 대권
12) consistent - a. (의견, 행동, 신념 등이) ...와 일치(조화, 양립)하는
13) clinic - n. 임상교실

courses attract 8 million participants, while driving ranges, 3 hole short courses, and instructional classes serve millions more.

Nature and purpose of the game

Golf is a game of skill and accuracy that demands concentration and emotional control. It is played by the sex from youth throughout life. A player sets her own pace, playing a fast and strenuous[14] 18 holes, or a leisurely 9 holes using a mechanical cart.

This vehicle[15] enables handicapped and aged persons to participate and benefit from good fellowship and exercise in the out-of-doors.

Golf is also an excellent competitive sport, for the United States Golf Association has developed a system for computing handicaps that allows poor, average, and skilled players to compete equitably.

The game consists of hitting a small, hard ball with selected clubs across various surface areas known as fairways[16], hazards[17], and roughs, to smooth patches of

---

14) strenuous - a. 정력적인, 열심인; 노력을 요하는, 격렬한
15) vehicle - n. 수송수단, 탈 것(자동차, 열차, 선박, 항공기, 우주선 등)
16) fairway - n. (골프) 티와 퍼팅그린 중간의 잔디구역
17) hazard - n. (골프) 장애지역

grass, known as greens. The object of the game is to use as few strokes as possible on each hole and over the entire course.

Although golf courses are laid out in units of 9 holes, most official courses have at least 18, and many have 27 or 36 holes. Par golf scores are based on 18 holes.

The 18 hole course is planned to balance play and avoid congestion[18]. It is divided into the "front nine" (out) and "back nine" (in). An 18 hole course includes 5200 to 7200 yards of playing area roughly equalized between the front nine and back nine. Each hole is assigned a par value, or an arbitrary standard of excellence, determined by the length and difficulty of the hole. This value allows a certain number of strokes to get to the green and two putts on the green.

An increasing number of golf clubs use the U.S.G.A. Course Rating System. The system is based on the fact that each course has peculiarities[19] which affect its playing difficulty. Factors such as yardage[20], topography[21], prevailing winds[22], size of green, and hazards of each hole are considered in determining a "difficulty rating." The differential established for the course, combined with a

---

18) congestion - n. 혼잡, 붐빔; (인구) 과잉, 밀집
19) peculiarity - n. 특색, 특수성; 특권
20) yardage - n. 골프코스의 타구 거리 따위의 야드로 잰 길이
21) topography - n. 지형도 작성; 지형학
22) prevailing wind - 효과적인 바람의 강한 흐름

player's individual handicap, creates an equality between players meeting on a strange course.

Course distances for par are:

Men	Women
Up to 250 yards, par 3	Up to 210 yards, par 3
251 to 470 yards, par 4	211 to 400 yards, par 4
471 to 600 yards, par 5	400 to 575 yards, par 5
601 yards and up, par 6	576 yards and up, par 6

Two, three, or four players may complete in one group. At the first tee, the order of teeing is decided by lot. Thereafter, the honor of playing first is awarded the player or team winning the preceding[23] hole. In case of a tie, the honor is awarded the individual or side that held it at the previous tee.

After the players have teed off, the person farthest away from the hole, whether on the fairway, in the rough, or on the green, shoots first. On the green the player farthest from the hole begins putting and continues until she "holes out." She may mark her ball only if her continued putting interferes with another player's line. After players "hole out," they move off the green and record their scores before going to the next teeing area.

---

23) preceding – a. 이전의; 바로 전의, 전술한

Facilities[24] and equipment

A golf course will eventually be the proving ground for all the skill and equipment of the golfer. Basic equipment includes clubs, balls, tees, and a carrying bag or rack. Other equipment may be desirable for comfort and skill improvement.

Clubs. The U.S.G.A. limits the golfer to the use of 14 clubs during a match. All 14 are not necessary for a beginning player, but even advanced players must be discriminating[25], for manufactures now design and produce a variety of specialized woods such as 5, 6, 31/2, and 41/2 as well as a choice of several wedges. A minimum[26] set of five clubs should be available to a student on a golf course.

Clubs are generally classified into two groups: woods and irons. The designation[27] originally referred to the composition of the clubheads; however, "woods" may have heads of plastic, magnesium, or laminated or persimon wood. Essentially, iron and wood clubs have the same parts.

The main parts of the club are the grip, shaft[28] and

---

24) facility - n. 쉬움, 평이(용이)함
25) discriminating - a. 식별하는; 식별력이 있는
26) minimum - n. 최소, 최소한도
27) designation - n. 지정, 명칭
28) shaft - n. (창, 망치 따위의) 자루, 손잡이

clubhead. The golfer holds the club by the leather or composition grip at the top of the shaft. A cap at the top of the handle protects the upper portion of the grip and secures[29] the wooden plug[30] to strength the hollow shaft. The shaft is a tension steel tube over which the grip is placed and into which the clubhead attaches.

The clubhead is below the neck of the club where the head and shaft join. It includes the sole, or the lower part of the club that rests on the ground; the heel, or the part nearest the shaft; the toe[31], or outer tip of the head; and clubface with its scored or grooved striking surface. Wooden clubs have a metal sole plate to protect the bottom as it swings across the ground. Iron clubs often have a metal flange[32] on the back of the head to give them additional weight.

Wooden clubs are named and numbered to designate their use:

Number 1- Driver: Has the largest head and longest shaft with a nearly vertical face. Used only for tee shots and gives a low, flat trajectory[33] with maximum distance to the ball.

---

29) secure - a. 안전한, 위험이 없는 v. 안전하게 하다, 굳게 하다
30) plug - n. 마개; 틀어막는 것
31) toe - n. (사람의) 발가락
32) flange - n. 날개, 모서리
33) trajectory - n. (투사물, 로켓, 천체 등이 그리는) 곡선, 호, 탄도, 궤도, 궤적, 비상경로

For the average woman it is 41 to 421/2 inches long and weighs 13 to 14 ounces[34].

Number 2- Brassie[35]: Used for long shots with good lies from the fairway and from the tee. The clubface has more loft, causing a ball to go higher into the air with less forward direction than when hit with a driver.

Number 3- Spoon[36]: Used for short tee shots and for long shots from the fairway and rough from mediocre[37] lies. More loft to the face and often a shorter shaft than those of number 1 or 2 woods, which allows better control.

Number 4- Cleek[38]: Used for long shots from a poor lie, as the smaller head and shallow face penetrate to the ball. It gives higher flight and less distance than 1, 2, or 3 woods.

Number 5- A popular club with women golfers, it has a small head and shallow face and is often used in preference to a number 1 or number 2 iron.

Iron clubs are informally grounded as long, medium, and short irons.

This classification refers to both the length of the shaft and to the ball flight distance attained by the use of each club. A cue to the beginner; "The larger the club number,

---

34) ounce - n. 중량 단위의 온스(상형에서는 28,3495그램)
35) Brassie - n. 2번 골프클럽의 고유명칭
36) Spoon - n. 3번 골프클럽의 고유명칭
37) mediocre - a. 좋지도 나쁘지도 않은, 보통의, 평범한; 2류의
38) Cleek - n. 4번 골프클럽의 고유명칭

the shorter the shaft, the more loft to the face: consequently, the higher and shorter the ball flight."

The long irons include numbers 1,2, and 3:

Number 1- Driving iron: Used for long, low, full shots from a good lie. The long shaft and straight face make it a difficult club for beginners. It is often replaced by a 3, 4 or 5 wood.

Number 2- Mid-iron: A utility club for comparatively long fairway and tee shots.

Number 3- Mid-mashie[39]: Used for less distance than a number 2 iron, but the loft of the face allows a stroke from a relatively bad lie.

The medium irons include numbers 4, 5, and 6:

Number 4- Mashie iron[40]: Used from the fairway and rough for medium distances, for occasional tee shots on short holes, and on "drag" strokes from the edge of the green.

Number 5- Mashie[41]: An excellent utility club for the beginner.

As the medium length club among all, at it is used from the fairway and rough, for pitching a ball high to the green, for pitch and run shots to the green when a safe approach is

---

39) Mid-mashie - n. 미드-매시 3번 아이언클럽의 고유명칭
40) Mashie iron - n. 매시 아이언 4번 클럽의 고유명칭
41) Mashie iron - n. 매시 아이언 5번 클럽의 고유명칭

desired, and as a tee club on short holes.

Number 6- Spade mashie[42]: Used from high rough, for pitch shots to the green, and from clean lies in a sand trap when distance is needed.

The short irons include numbers 7, 8, 9, and the wedges:

Number 7- Mashie niblick[43]: Used for short pitch shots from fairway and traps and over trees and obstacles.

Number 8- Pitching niblick[44]: Used for quickrising shots over hazards or as an approach from the fairway. An excellent club when obstacles prevent a follow-through.

Number 9- Niblick[45]: The iron with the greatest loft. Used from deep rough and short approaches to the green.

Wedge: Either pitching or sand wedge. The heavy, flanged clubhead has a very slanted face and is used to loft the ball from sand, high grass, and other hazards.

The putter is an essential club for all golfers. In a category of its own, this short-shafted club with a straight face is used to stroke the ball over the smooth surface of the green.

Balls. Golf balls are constructed of liquid, rubber, steel, or

---

42) Spade mashie - n. 스페이드 매시 아이언 6번 클럽의 고유명칭
43) Mashie niblick - n. 매시 니브릭 아이언 7번 클럽의 고유명칭
44) Pitching niblick - n. 피칭 니브릭 아이언 8번 클럽의 고유명칭
45) Niblick - n. 니브릭 아이언 9번 클럽의 고유명칭

plastic centers surrounded by tightly bound rubber yarn and encased in a balata rubber[46] cover of dimpled design and painted white. They range in price from approximately 35c to $1.50. The less expensive repainted or factory-rejected balls have thick covers that decrease the chances of cutting the ball, allowing inexpensive play. The more expensive balls are designed for maximum accuracy and distance. Personal balls should be clearly marked for rapid identification.

Practice balls of plastic, cotton, felt, and woolen yarn[47] are available for indoor and backyard use.

Tee and Tee Mats. Tees are used to elevate the balls for the first drive on each hole. Inexpensive wooden or plastic tees should be selected, as tees are often broken or lost.

If practice space is available indoors or on the lawn mats are desirable. Heavy duty rubber mats with rubber tees, are satisfactory for tee shots, but coco[48] mats are better for iron club practice, as they "give" with the impact of the hands and wrists and allow the clubhead to contact the ball below ground level.

Strips[49] of close pile carpeting, or commercial indoor

---

46) balata rubber - n. 발라타(서인도 제도산의 열대나무)의 고무

47) yarn - n. 털실, 모사(woolen)

48) coco - n. 식물 (코코) 야자수(coconut palm) 열매

49) strip - n. (헝겊, 종이, 널빤지 따위의) 길고 가느다란 조각

turfs[50], can serve for indoor putting surfaces.

Bag. A light fabric[51] "Sunday" bag is ideal for the beginning golfer with limited equipment. The more durable[52] and attractive leather or fabric bag, with shoe and ball pockets, a carry strap and handle, and a hood, is a heavy burden for the woman golfer with a full set of clubs who cannot afford regular caddy service.

Golf carts. A number of pull carts are available for purchase or rental. The light-weight pocket bag built on a cart is ideal for the golfer with limited clubs; others prefer a sturdy collapsible cart[53] that carries a bag and rain gear and offers such accessories as a seat and score card rack. Some courses prohibit the use of pull carts and insist on caddies or power-driven golfer carts.

Costume[54]. Shoe that offer comfort and help to maintain balance and stability while swinging are a valuable part of a golfer's equipment. Some players find rubber-soled canvas shoes satisfactory, but many insist on spikes. Spikes can be

---

50) turfs - n. (집합적) 잔디; 뗏장
51) fabric - n. 직물, 천편물; 직물의 짜임새, 바탕
52) durable - a. 오래 견디는, 튼튼한; 영속성이 있는, 내구력이 있는
53) a sturdy collapsible cart - n. 튼튼한 접이식 이륜 경마차
54) costume - n. 복장, 의상

placed on flat-soled oxfords if an investment in golf shoes is inappropriate.

Jewelry should not be worn, as rings may injure the hands and the delicate[55] mechanism of wrist watches may be ruined by the stroking impact.

When in doubt[56] about club regulations concerning dress, wear a semifull skirt and a neat, loose fitting blouse, or a manufacturer's golf dress, all of which are comfortable when walking and swinging a club. Long walking shorts or slacks are acceptable on most courses.

Accessories and Gadgets[57]. There are many accessories for gloves, full or half, which aid in gripping and prevent calluses; an umbrella for the inevitable thundershowers; and a shade hat. Other useful items include stroke counters to aid the novice[58] in keeping her score, ball markers for use on the green, and ball holders worn on the belt to eliminate bulging pockets.

Commercial gadgets designed to improve basic skills are numerous. Such items[59] as a golf grove to correct improper grip, a plastic sleeve[60] to prevent bending the elbow on the

---

55) delicate - a. 섬세한, 우아한, 고운
56) in doubt - 의심하여 망설이고
57) gadget - n. 도구, 부속품
58) novice - n. 신참자, 초심자; 풋내기
59) item - n. 항목, 조목, 조항, 품목
60) sleeve - n. 소매, 소맷자락

backswing, and elbow down may have value, but should be prescribed by an instructor who analyzes the problems of your swing. These aids are not permitted in competitive play.

Basic skills

All skills are described in term of a right-handed player.

The skills and movements are applicable to left-handed players, but the terms left and right must be interchanged[61] when developing or analyzing a skill.

Grip. The positioning of the hands is of initial importance, for the hands are the only connection between the body and the ball, working through the club. A sound grip serves to place the hands so that they return to their original position to contact the ball.

The same basic grip is used for all clubs except the putter. Three grips are commonly used by golfers: the overlap, the interlock, and the natural, or "baseball." Although several championship golfers use the interlocking and natural grips, for most women the overlapping technique assures[62] close

---

61) interchange - vt. 교환하다, 주고받다; 교체(대체)시키다
62) assure - vt. ...에게 보증하다, ...에게 보장하다

hands and hinged[63] wrist action.

To assume[64] the overlapping grip the clubhead rests on the ground in square position, shaft pointing toward the golfer. The extended left hand is placed slightly over the top of the shaft lie diagonally[65] across the hand in a combination palm and finger grip. The end of the shaft extends and inch or more beyond the hand toward the body. The grip is secured by the last three fingers, with the thumb and index finger forming a "V" line.

This solid and closed line points toward the chin and right shoulder.

With the left hand thumb[66] to the right of the shaft, the thumb and index finger exert[67] a slight gripping pressure. Looking down the shaft, the golfer should see no more than three knuckle[68] joints.

The right arm swings freely until the right hand reaches below the left to grip the club entirely in the fingers. The palm of the right hand is squarely[69] facing the right side of the club shaft.

---

63) hinge - n. 돌쩌귀, 경첩 v. 돌쩌귀를 달다
64) assume - v. (태도, 임무, 책임 따위를) 취하다, 떠맡다
65) diagonally - ad. 대각선으로, 비스듬히
66) thumb - n. 엄지손가락
67) exert - vt. (힘, 지력 따위를) 발휘하다, 쓰다
68) knuckle - n. 손가락 관절(마디)
69) squarely - ad. 네모꼴로, 네모지게; 직각으로

In closing the right hand around the club, the left thumb fits snugly[70] into the natural diagonal hollow[71] of the right palm (under the butt of the right thumb). Overlap the little finger of the right hand by hooking it around the large knuckle of the left index finger. The next three fingers grasp the shaft as the index finger spreads to a trigger[72] position so that there is a space between the index and second fingers. The "V" line formed by the right thumb and index finger is solid and closed and points in the same direction of chin and right shoulder. With both hands close together and working as a unit, power and control are attained.

Putting grip. The individuality of putting begins with the grip. Many golfers use the same grip as they use for other clubs;

others use a baseball, crosshand, reverse overlap, or two-hand molded grip, in which both hands and thumb are molded together at the top of the shaft.

The reverse overlap grip is recommended for beginners, as the hands are placed on the club in a manner resembling[73] the Vardon grip.

---

70) snugly - a. (장소 따위가) 아늑한, 편안한, 포근하고 따스한, 안락한
71) hollow - a. 속이 빈; 우묵한
72) trigger - n. (총의) 방아쇠
73) resemble - vt. ...와 비슷하다; 닮다

The right hand is placed a hand span[74] from the top of the club with the thumb pointed directly down the front of the shaft toward the clubhead. The line formed by the thumb and index finger points toward the right shoulder. The left hand is placed above the right with the palm facing in the direction opposite from that of the palm of the right hand. The back of the left hand faces the line of the putt.

The thumb is down the front of the shaft. The index finger of the left hand overlaps the little finger of the right hand. The line of the thumb and index finger[75] of the left hand should point in the direction of the left shoulder.

The left hand, now firmly holding the club-more in the palm than the fingers-does most of the work. The pressure of the grip in the right hand is exerted with the thumb and index finger for control. This grip permits a hinged wrist action.

Stance and address. A firm, comfortable stance assures the balance necessary for all strokes, except putting, weight is equally distributed on both feet between the balls of the feet and the heels, the toes are pointed outward, and the feet are placed comfortably apart but never more than shoulder width. The body is fairly erect, with knees flexed.

---

74) span - n. 한 뼘(엄지와 새끼손가락을 편 길이; 보통 9인치)
75) index finger - n. 집게손가락

The body curves as if it is sitting on a ball. With eyes on the ball, extend the left arm so that it is firm and straight. The arms hang but do not reach so as to pull the body off balance.

The distance one stands from the ball depends on the length of the club used. Sole the club directly behind the ball so that the bottom is evenly[76] placed on the turf and the face points directly along the desired line of flight.

There are three general stances which a golfer assumes for a designated[77] stroke:

Square or parallel stance. The feet are parallel to, and equally distant from, the imaginary[78] line of flight of the ball. White the knees, hips, and shoulders parallel to the flight line, this is a good beginning stance, as it gives a feeling of balanced swing motion with an equally balanced swing and follow-through. It is the most commonly used stance for long and medium irons.

Open stance. The left foot is drawn back from the imaginary flight line. The body is turned slightly toward the direction of ball flight. With the right hip forward a restricted[79] body rotation in the backswing results, thus

---

76) evenly – ad. 평탄하게, 평평하게; 공평하게; 대등하게; 고르게
77) designate – vt. 가르키다, 지시(지적)하다, 표시(명시)하다, 나타내다
78) imaginary – a. 상상의, 가상의
79) restrict – vt. 제한하다, 한정하다; 금지하다, 제지하다

allowing the arms to stay closer to the body for a more controlled stroke. The open stance is used primarily for short irons, chipping[80], and pitching, when less distance and power but greater accuracy are needed. It may be used for intentional slices.

<u>Closed stance.</u> The right foot is drawn back from the flight line, thus turning the body from the target and increasing backswing rotation. This stance is used for maximum power from the tee and on some fairway shots, as well as for an intentional hook shot[81].

<u>Body-ball position.</u> The position of the body and the club in relation to the ball greatly affects ball flight. Basically, the longer the club the fuller the swing arc[82]. The farther one stands from the ball, the flatter the swing; the shorter the club, the closer one stands to the ball and the more upright the swing.

When the ball is contacted as near as possible to the bottom of the swing, the more perfect will be the loft[83] for which the clubhead was designed. To get this proper position with irons, hit down on the ball, which is placed an inch or two to the right of the bottom of the swing arc.

---

80) chip - v. 잘게 썰다, 깎다, 자르다, 쪼개다
81) hook shot - n. 좌곡구 샷(왼쪽 곡선으로 치는 타법)
82) arc - n. 호, 호형, 궁형
83) loft - n. 골프채 두부의 경사; (공을) 올려치기

The point on the swing arc at which the ball is hit greatly affects ball spin. A forward spin, causing low ball flight and increased forward roll on the ground, results from a blow as the clubhead is traveling upward. A horizontal[84] blow at the center of the swing arc results in a slight backspin, as the ball is hit below center.

A definite backspin is caused if the clubhead hits the ball before the center of the swing arc is reached, for the club continues downward[85] across the back of the ball.

Generally, tee shots and wood shots are made from a closed or square stance with the ball placed forward of center for a horizontal or upward impact of the club. The long and medium irons are most often played from a square stance off or near the center or the body. The length of the club shaft determines the golfer's relation to the ball, but the arms are easy, not forcibly[86] reaching, and the wrists are down and firm. With shorter irons, the golfer moves closer to the ball, opens her stance, moves the feet closer together, and plays the ball off-center or right of center of the body for more loft and less roll.

Swing. An efficient swing is based on balance, rhythm,

---

84) horizontaⅠ- a. 수평의, 평평한, 가로의; 수평선의
85) downward - a. 내려가는, 내리받이의; 아래쪽으로의, 아래로 향한
86) forcibly - ad. 강제적으로; 강력히, 세차게, 힘차게

and a square clubhead position throughout.

Although the total swing must be learned as a unit, the basic ingredients[87] can be identified for analysis.

Assuming a proper stance with weight distributed and feet comfortably spread, exert a slight gripping pressure on the inside of the right foot and press the right thigh[88] toward the center of the body.

This is inclined forward slightly dropped so that the arm can reach properly and eventually bend on the backswing. The upper arms rest slightly against the sides of the body with the left arm fully extended but not stiff[89] or tense[90]. The hands are even with or slightly ahead of the ball.

The backswing is a one-piece move away from the ball. The left shoulder initiates the coordinated movement by turning down and moving under the chin[91]. The hips rotate toward the right, with the spine and head serving as an axis[92]. The weight shifts across the left foot to the inside of the right foot. The left knee relaxes and bends toward the right knee. The left heel is unweighted and in a full swing it may be raised about an inch from the ground. During the

---

87) ingredients - n. (혼합물의) 성분, 합성분; 구성요소, 요인
88) thigh - n. 넓적다리
89) stiff - a. 뻣뻣한, 딱딱한, 경직된, 굳은
90) tense - a. (신경, 감정이) 긴장한; 긴박(절박)한, 긴장시키는
91) chin - n. 턱, 턱끝
92) axis - n. 굴대, 축

pivot the arms and shoulders pull the club backward along the flight line and upward. The shoulders turn as the upper body pivots with the hips.

As the arms reach approximately waist height, the wrists cock with no deliberate[93] effort and the arms continue in an upward arc.

The left arm and right leg remain firm, with the right elbow bent and pointing downward. The head remains stationary[94].

At the top of the full swing, the body is in coiled readiness[95] with the club shaft approximately horizontal to the ground.

The shoulders are turned 90 degrees; the hips 45 degrees. The palm of the right hand is under the shaft; the right elbow is pointing to the ground with the line from the right armpit[96] to the elbow parallel to the ground.

A shift of weight back to the left foot initiates the downswing. The weight shift may be accomplished by pulling the club down sharply with the left hand or by sliding or turning the hips to the left. Beginners seem to find it easier to concentrate on a vigorous push off the right foot

---

93) deliberate - a. 계획적인, 숙고한 뒤의, 고의의
94) stationary - a. 움직이지 않은, 정지된
95) readiness - n. 준비, 채비; 용이; 신속
96) armpit - n. 겨드랑이

to the left. A proper shift allows the right elbow to move toward the body as the left hip leads the body and pulls the arms into the hitting area. Halfway[97] through the downswing, the weight has returned to address position, the hips are square, but the shoulders are still turned 45 degrees. The right shoulder then turns under the chin and below the left shoulder. As the arms and wrists come to the impact area the wrists uncock to strike the ball at the bottom of the swing arc. The golfer hits against a firm left side.

A key point in the downswing is the action of the right shoulder. At the moment of ball impact the chin is digging[98] into the right shoulder.

The clubhead follows the line of intended flight until the right arm is fully extended in handshaking position.

As weight continues to shift to the left side with the right foot pushing from the toes, the left elbow bends and the right hand takes over the club. The hips turn naturally with the turn of the arms and shoulders. At the completion[99] of the swing the right side is fully released, the weight is on the left foot, the hands are high with the left palm under the shaft and the left elbow pointed toward the ground. The

97) halfway – a. 도중의, 중간의
98) digging – n. 파기, 채굴, 채광
99) completion – n. 완성, 성취, 완결; (목적의) 달성

head has turned and the body is facing[100] the target in a balanced position.

Fractional[101] swings. The power of a full swing is neither necessary nor desirable for some shots and clubs. Basically, fractional swings are but segments[102] of the full swing and are frequently used with short irons. As the swing is shortened, the club is shortened proportionately[103] by gripping farther down on the leather.

Quarter swing. The hips initiate a weight shift, rather than a true rotation. The clubhead follows, going away from the ball until the arms are outside the right leg; then the wrists cock[104], bringing the club parallel to the ground. The downswing and follow-through carry the club to a position parallel to the ground on the left side of the body.

Half swing. Executed[105] by a rotation slightly deeper than that of the quarter swing, the backswing are continues until the cap of the grip points toward the ground. The follow-through is the same length as the backswing.

Three-quarter swing. This is executed like the full swing but less depth is taken in the ascending[106] and

---

100) facing - n. 면함, 향함, (집의) 향
101) fractional - a. 단편의; 얼마 안 되는; (수학) 분수의; (화학) 분류의
102) segment - n. 단편, 조각; 부분, 구획
103) proportionately - ad. 균형잡히게 하는, 비례를 이루는, 적응하게 하는
104) cock - v. (총의) 공이치기를 당기다, (때리려고 주먹 따위를) 뒤로 끌다
105) execute - vt. (계획 따위를) 실행하다, 실시하다; 수행하다
106) ascend - v. 올라가다, 기어오르다; (공중 따위로) 오르다

descending[107] arcs. At the top of the backswing the clubhead points to 2 o' clock; on the following-through it points toward 10 o' clock.

Playing wood shots

1. Use a square or slightly closed stance with feet 10 to 14 inches apart, depending on comfort.

2. Use a full swing for maximum power.

3. When driving from the tee, play the ball off of forward heel or toe, depending on the bottom point of the swing.

4. Play fairway shots toward the center of the body.

Playing long and medium iron shots

1. Use square stance for normal flight.

2. Stand slightly closer to irons than woods so that the swing will be more upright.

3. The body is close to the ball; the arms close to the body.

4. Use a fractional swing for distance desired.

---

107) descend - v. 내리다, 내려가다

Chip shot. A chip (also called a pitch and run) is made when the ball is close to the green and there is a 5 yard unobstacled[108] approach to the green. A chip should carry to the green and roll the rest of the way to the hole[109].

1. Use a number 4, 5, 6, or 7 iron; occasionally[110] an 8 or 9 iron.

2. Keep the feet close together and the weight on the left foot as the ball is played in line with the left heel. There should be little body motion or weight transfer[111].

3. Grip club low on the handle, hands ahead of club to limit loft. The left hand controls as both wrists remain firm.

4. Use a short, rhythmical backswing. Stroke the ball crisply. The right palm faces the target throughout.

5. The follow-through is low.

Pitch shot. The pitch carries the ball through the air in a high approach toward the green, where it stops quickly upon contact with the ground.

1. Select a wedge[112] or 9 iron.

2. Use an open stance close to the ball with the right elbow close to the right hip.

---

108) unobstacled - a. 장애(방해)물이 없는, 지장이 없는
109) hole - n. 구멍; 틈
110) occasionally - ad. 이따금, 가끔
111) transfer - vt. 옮기다, 운반(이동)하다
112) wedge - n. (골프) 쳐올리기 용의 아이언 클럽(웨지)

3. Use minimum body action with a fractional swing.

4. Hit the ball several inches ahead of the bottom of the swing arc (a descending blow) to impart backspin so that it will stop when landing.

5. Follow through with clubhead pointing toward target.

Run-up shot. The run-up is similar to the pitch and run but is taken farther from the green. The ball is hit with a 6 or 7 iron and played to travel about one-half the distance to the green in the air, hit level. firm terrain[113], and roll onto the green and toward the cup.

Bunker shots. The chip shot and the blast[114] are the fundamental strokes for getting out of a sand trap[115]. The texture[116] of the sand and the lie of the ball determine the shot. A chip may be used when the ball is resting on top of the sand.

A number 6 or 7 iron may be used in a short approach. The club, however, must not be grounded or touch the sand on the backswing.

The explosive[117] shot is the safest when the ball is

---

113) terrain – n. 지대, 지역; 지형; 지세
114) blast – n. 한바탕의 바람, 돌풍
115) trap – n. 올가미, 함정; 덫
116) texture – n. 조직, 구조; (피부, 목재, 암석 등의) 결
117) explosive – a. 폭발하기 쉬운, 폭발성의

buried[118] or must rise over a bank.

1. Select a sand wedge or number 9 iron. Open the club face slightly (angle it backward).

2. Play the ball in line with the left (forward) heel.

3. Anchor the feet and aim an inch or two behind the ball. Take sand as a cushion to loft the ball.

4. Take a full swing; start the clubhead back at an angle outside the line of flight. Swing through the ball, cutting across the direction line, and follow through completely.

Putting. Putting is the most individualized skill of golf; its success also depends largely on the player's state of mind. Although the criterion[119] of a good putt is its effectiveness, the following techniques may help the beginner.

1. Use the reverse overlap grip.

2. Take a square stance, with the feet 10 to 12 inches apart. Bend from the waist so that the eyes are directly over the ball. Look the stance.

3. Position the ball off the instep of the left foot.

4. Keep the hands even with the ball, with the right elbow resting comfortably on the right hipbone[120], the left elbow barely[121] touching the left side.

---

118) bury – vt. 묻다, (흙 따위로) 덮다
119) criterion – n. (비판, 판단의) 기준, 표준; 특징
120) hipbone – n. 좌골, 무명골
121) barely – ad. 가까스로, 간신히, 겨우, 거의 ...않다

5. To execute the wrist action putt, the head, hips, and shoulders remain steady as the hands and wrists take a short controlled backswing. To execute an arm action putt or firm wrist putt, the head and hips are steady as the arms swing from the shoulders. The elbows remain close to the sides.

6. Two methods of striking the ball are commonly used. In both, the clubhead accelerates[122] at the moment of impact. The stroke putt is a long, smooth stroke with backswing and follow-through of equal distance; the tap putt results from a swing that crispy[123] contacts the ball and ends in a short follow-through. This is often called a "punch putt."

7. Bring the clubhead straight back, then through the ball, following through directly toward the hole.

8. Keep the putter blade close to the green throughout the stroke.

Putts account for approximately half the strokes in a round of par golf; therefore, putting deserves concentration and practice.

Line up a putt by determining the distance to the hole, the slope[124] of the green, the grain[125] of the grass, and

---

122) accelerate- vt. 빨리 하다, 가속하다
123) crispy- a. 파삭파삭한, 딱딱하고 부서지기 쉬운
124) slope- n. 경사면, 비탈
125) grain- n. 기질, 성미, 성질

ultimately the course of the ball to the hole. It is helpful to pick a spot about 6 inches along the imaginary ball course and concentrate on rolling the ball over that spot[126].

Badminton

Badminton originated from the ancient game battledore[127] and shuttlecock played in Siam and China over 2000 years ago. A modified version of this sport, known as "Poona." caught the attention and enthusiasm[128] of British Army officers stationed in India, who around 1870 brought the game home to England. The Duke of Beaufort gave real impetus to the game at his eastate, Badminton House, in the rural hamlet of Badminton in Gloucestershire. The game spread rapidly throughout the world and reached the United States via Canada. Since 1929 it has gained thousands of enthusiastic players and spectators in this country. Numerous tournaments are sponsored by the American

126) spot - n. 장소, 지점; 현장
127) battledore - n. 깃털재기 채, 빨래방망이
128) enthusiasm - n. 열심, 열중, 열광, 의욕, 열의

Badminton Association, and many individuals subscribe[129] to "Bird Chatter[130]," the official publication of this organization. The game is taught and played in many of our secondary schools and colleges.

As a coeducational and family activity, badminton has no equal. It is a sport with great appeal for all ages, as well as for those of varying skill levels and degrees of physical stamina.

Although the beginner can quickly learn to hit the bird back and forth across the net, it is the advanced player, who has mastered game strategy[131] and bird placement, who receives the greatest satisfaction from the game.

Since badminton requires little space and can be played outdoors or indoors on an imperfect surface, and since accident possibilities and game hazards are minimal and needed equipment is inexpensive, it is an ideal activity for schools, camps, organizations, and backyard family fun.

Nature and purpose of the sport

Badminton can be played as a singles or doubles game with one or two players on a side. The object of this racket

---

129) subscribe - vt. (기부 따위를) 기명 승낙하다, 기부하다; 응모하다, 신청하다
130) bird chatter - 새의 지저귐
131) strategy - n. 용병학, 병법; (대규모의) 전략, 전술, 책략

game is to serve and hit the shuttlecock, or bird, across a net (5 feet from the floor at its center and 5 feet and 1 inch at the sides) with such skill and accuracy that the opponent[132] is unable to return the shot.

Facilities and equipment

Badminton rackets weigh between 41/2 and 6 ounces and are approximately 26 inches long.

The average handle size is 31/2 to 33/4 inches. The body of the delicate[133] racket is made of aluminum, fiberglass, plastic, or wood and strung with nylon, gut, or linen. Advanced players prefer wooden rackets strung with nylon or gut. When not in use, all such rackets should be kept in a press and hung in a dry place. A badminton cart with multiple presses is recommended for both proper storage and ease of distribution of rackets for class use.

Shuttlecocks may have 14 to 16 goose feathers in a plastic or cock base covered with fine leather. Cork is best for skilled players. The best birds[134] are stitched[135] in three

---

132) opponent - a. 반대하는, 적대하는
　　　　　　　 n. (경기, 논쟁 따위의) 적, 상대; 대항자
133) delicate - a. 섬세한, 우아한, 고운
134) bird - n. (배드민턴의) 깃털 공
135) stitch - vt. 바느질하다; 꿰매어 꾸미다; ...에 자수하다

places to keep the 16 feather spines[136] and quills[137] straight. Before using the more costly birds, beginners may be taught with wool or cotton practice balls, or with fleece[138] balls homemade of yarn or obtained commercially, or with birds made of synthetic materials and chicken feathers. Students should be cautioned against damaging it by kicking or stepping on it or putting it into play with overhead strokes. All feathered birds should be kept in a humidifier[139] at a temperature between 60 and 65° F. and a humidity of 70 to 75 per cent. A modified humidifier can be made by placing a small tin can filled with water on a well filled sponge in a larger can.

Place a wire screen over the smaller can and scatter the birds over it; then cover both cans to retain the moisture[140].

The net should be made of fine meshed[141] cord, edged on top with 3 inch white tape. It should be kept folded and stored in a dry place when not in use.

Rubber-soled tennis shoes or sneakers[142] are required for safe indoor play and are also recommended for outdoor use.

---

136) spine - n. 가시모양의 돌기
137) quill - n. (날개깃, 꼬리 따위의 튼튼한) 큰 깃
138) fleece - n. 양털
139) humidify - vt. 축이다, 축축하게 하다
140) moisture - n. 습기, 수분
141) meshed - vt. 그물로 잡다, 그물에 걸리다
142) sneaker - n. 고무바닥의 운동화

Basic skills

The grip. A flexible wrist snap is imperative[143] for efficient stroking on both the forehand and backhand. This is best accomplished on the forehand by grasping the handle with a handshake grip while the racket face is at right angles to the ground. The fingers are spread slightly apart, with the forefinger[144] extended diagonally and slightly bent behind the handle. The thumb is cocked and wrapped around the inside of the handle, exerting pressure against the forefinger. The handle rests at the base of the fingers but not in the palm, with the "V" formed by the thumb and forefinger on the inside top of the handle and in line with the racket head.

Swing the racket back and forth, snapping the wrist to get the feel of the necessary quick, definite movement.

The backhand grip is similar to the Eastern backhand grip in tennis. To gain the backhand from a forehand grip position, hold the racket by the throat[145] with the left hand and turn the right hand to the left so that the first knuckle is on top of the racket handle. Extend the thumb diagonally up and back of the handle. The "V" line formed by the thumb and forefinger is somewhat behind the racket when

---

143) imperative - a. 피할 수 없는, 절박한, 긴요한
144) forefinger - n. 집게손가락
145) throat - n. 테니스 라켓의 목부분

held in front of the player. The advanced player will notice that the backhand grip results in a slight wrist cock as the arm is brought across the body in preparation for a backhand stroke.

The Forehand drive. This stroke, which is similar to throwing a softball, is a flowing, free movement in which the follow-through plays an important part. It is a natural movement used when returning the bird from the right side of the body. The head of the racket should be kept higher than the wrist, and the left foot is brought forward, the body leaning[146] slightly sideward toward the net. The backswing should start at the same time the left foot is brought forward.

Simultaneous[147] with a pivotal shift of the body weight from the rear to the forward foot, the bent elbow leads the flexed wrist into the stroking area. The wrist should be slightly ahead of the racket head and snapped at the moment of contact. If the player wants to hit the bird upward, she should swing low, then up to it, whereas to hit it downward, the forward swing is in a downward arc. The arm should be extended and relaxed and the bird hit

---

146) leaning - n. 경사; 경향, 성향; 기호, 편애
147) simultaneous - a. 동시에, 동시에 일어나는, 동시에 존재하는

squarely[148] in the racket center by a quick wrist flick[149].

The backhand drive. The backhand drive is made with the right shoulder facing the net and the racket held with a backhand grip. As the bird is hit with the reverse side of the racket, the weight is shifted with the feet in a stride[150] position from the rear to the forward foot. When the bird is played in front of the body, the thumb may be held so that it rests flat against the nonhitting side of the racket for more power and better control.

The Serve. The racket is held with a forehand grip. The shuttle should be struck in front of the body with the full arm stretched for a relaxed but forceful movement.

With feet in stride position, the body weight shifts from the forward foot to back, then is returned to forward as the bird is hit. The wrist flick, forward arc swing and follow-through should be easy, natural movements. There is very little follow-through on a short serve. Beginners should drop the bird from the thumb and index finger, held at the extreme feather tip, and play it in front of the forward foot.

---

148) squarely - ad. 네모꼴로, 네모지게; 직각으로
149) flick - n. (매, 채찍 따위로) 찰싹(탁) 때리기; (손가락 끝으로) 가볍게 튀기기
150) stride - n. 큰 걸음, 활보; 한 걸음의 폭
　　　　　 v. 큰 걸음으로 걷다, 활보하다

Advanced players may master the toss serve by throwing the bird slightly into the air and contacting it with a well timed forward stroke. The majority[151] of serves in singles should be high and deep; in doubles they should be low and land just inside the service court or on a boundary[152] line. To be a legal serve, the bird must be contacted below the waist with no part of the racket higher than the server's hand.

The long high serve should be used most often in singles. It is basically the same as the underhand clear shot and is used to force the opponent into the back court, thus giving the server added time to get into the best court position for offensive play. For this long serve, the bird may be tossed or dropped well in front of the server. She should aim toward the ceiling, and her body should lean slightly forward as she sweeps[153] her arm swiftly forward in a long, fast, swinging movement to contact the bird.

If she chooses to drop the bird, she should do so at the end of the backswing. If the toss release in used, the bird should be thrown to the right of the forward foot as the backswing begins.

The short serve is best for doubles play and is used to

---

151) majority - n. 대부분, 대다수
152) boundary - n. 한계, 범위, 영역
153) sweep - vt. (먼지 따위를) 털다, 쓸다, 청소하다

force the receiver to hit the bird up high on the return so that the opponents can use a smash or quick kill shot to gain a point. It can also be used sometimes as a surprise[154] or to change game pace. In this stroke, the bird should barely[155] clear the net and be placed close to the net at either corner of the receiver's court. The bird should be stroked, rather than hit, with little follow-through. In order to deceive[156] the receiver, the backswing should be forceful. The bird should be guided carefully so that it barely clears the net and gives the impression[157] that it will not do so.

The driven serve is used most often in doubles (sometimes, too, in singles for a surprise) and is used to deceive the receiver into thinking that the serve will be a fault[158] by landing in the wrong back court. Although the footwork and basic motions are the same as for other serves, the follow-through should be toward the net at chest height, and the bird should be hit hard enough to land deep in the service court and aimed to land close to the midline[159] of the service court.

---

154) surprise - n. 놀람, 경악
155) barely - ad. 가까스로, 간신히, 겨우, 거의 ...않다
156) deceive - vt. 속이다, 기만하다, 현혹시키다
157) impression - n. 인상, 감명, 감상
158) fault - n. (구기) 서브의 실패(무효)
159) midline - n. (신체 따위의) 중선, 중간선

Footwork and the ready position. The player must learn how to move quickly over the court, carrying her weight on the balls of her feet with easy, relaxed knees and posture. The right foot should be back on the forehand drive, and the body should face the right sideline, with the left foot forward. On the stroke, body weight should shift from the back to the forward foot. On the backhand drive, this pattern is reversed. The player faces the left sideline, and body weight is forward foot while stroking. The sweep, force and racket movement speed should all be increased and the knees more deeply bent on shots which require more force.

The player should face the net for the ready position. Her left foot should be slightly forward. The racket should be held a bit above eye level in front of her body, and its head should be pointed up and toward her opponent. Beginners should practice changing quickly from the ready position to hitting an imaginary[160] bird forehand, backhand, above the head, and below the knees in quick, swishing[161] movements.

The overhead stroke. On this shot the bird is hit above the head to the right of the body for the forehead and to the left

160) imaginary - a. 상상의, 가상의
161) swish - vt. 획 소리를 내다, 획 움직이다 vi. 휘두르다, 획 소리내다

for the backhand overhand stroke.

The feet are held shoulder width apart in stride position. As the bird is contacted, body weight shifts from the rear to the forward foot.

The arm is slightly bent and is extended when the bird is hit slightly in front of the body with a forceful wrist flick. The racket follow-through makes a half circle. Quick judgement, timing and accuracy are required to hit the approaching bird at least six inches in front of the body and to bring it down just over the net and well placed in the opponent's court[162].

The round-the-head shot. Similar to the overhead stroke, this one is stronger and often more effective. The narrow stride stance and shift of weight from the rear to the forward foot are similar to those used in most shots, except that the weight should end well balanced on the left foot. Contact is made with the bird above the shoulder and around the head on the left side by extending the bent stroking arm in order to hit the bird on the forehand side.

---

162) in the opponent's court – 상대방의 코트에서

Strokes classified by bird flight

The high clear[163]. Played either by the forehand or backhand, the high clear is a defensive stroke used to gain time, to move the opponent into the back court, or to change game pace.

The bird is played just as it is in either the forehand or backhand and should land far in the back court after sailing high into the air. It is similar to the tennis lob[164].

The drive. This attacking stroke should barely clear the net. It can be played with either the forehand or backhand, usually down one side, to force the opponent to switch[165] court sides. The bird can best be controlled for this stroke at shoulder height but can be also played successfully from knee level. Variance[166] in bird speed must be mastered[167] in order to use this shot most effectively.

The Drop shot. The name of this stroke best describes it, for it is a shot that causes the bird to drop sharply, close to the net, into the opponent's front court. Played like any

---

163) high clear - n. (배드민턴) 클리어 샷(호를 그리며 상대방 등 뒤, 엔드라인 안으로 떨어지는 플라이트)

164) lob - n. (스포츠) 로브 (테니스 등) 높고 완만한 공을 보냄

165) switch - vt. 바꾸다, 전환하다, 돌리다

166) variance - n. 변화, 변동, 변천

167) master - vt. ...에 숙달하다, ...에 정통하다

other shot, it requires control and placement ability. It is used as a surprise attack to change game pace, or to fool the opponent who expects a drive or clear into the back court and has moved back for it and thus out of position. Cross court drop shots are especially effective. Overhand strokes wisest when close to the net.

The smash. The smash is used more in doubles than in singles. It is best played in midcourt[168] and should be aimed directly at the opponent, to her weakest defensive body side (usually backhand for left-handed players), or at open court spaces. It should be a powerful, fast stroke and can be best done with a forehand. In the forehand smash the left foot should be ahead and the racket swung[169] far back behind the head and shoulder by a flexible wrist. The bird should be hit ahead of the forward left foot and weight put into the stroke by a forceful body shift as contact is made with the bird. The term "smash" describes both the stroke and how to do it correctly.

The net or hairpin shot. Played close to the net, this shot can send the bird just barely over it, diagonally across it, or

---

168) midcourt – n. 코트의 중앙
169) swung – swing의 과거, 과거분사
　　　　vi. 흔들리다, 흔들거리다; 진동하다

far into the back court as a high clear. The bird should be hit near the net top, and the racket held face up by the extended arm as it gently taps the shuttlecock with a slight wrist action. Careful aiming, together with this restricted wrist motion, will direct the bird most effectively. The net clear is similar to the drop shot but is done with a delayed, more pronounced wrist flick. This stroke is ideal for changing game pace, gaining time, wearing the opponent down, and restricting the possibility of any diagonal or outward angles to a returned shot.

Basketball

Basketball is truly the "All-American game." Created by Dr. James Naismith to fulfill a class assignment[170], basketball has grown into the most popular participating and spectator team sport in the country. The game as originally played in Y.M.C.A. class at Springfield, Massachusetts, was a simple, 13 rule, indoor winter sport that served the same team

---

170) assignment - n. 할당, 할당된 몫

purposes as football during the fall and baseball in the spring. Originally, a large number of men composed two teams and were allowed to bat, pass, and throws in an attempt to get the ball into peach[171] basket goals nailed to each end of the gymnasium balcony.

Although women were not in Dr. Naismith's original plans, they quickly saw the value of the game. A short two weeks after the game was introduced, a group of women teachers asked to play.

The game spread rapidly, but misinterpretations[172] and misunderstandings of the rules led to confusion[173] across the nation.

A rule misinterpretation by Miss Clara Baer in 1893 at Newcomb College in New Orleans ultimately developed the three division court game. The first rules committee met in 1899 and accepted the three game.

The first basketball guide for women was edited[174] by Senda Berenson and eliminated snatching and batting of the ball, limited the dribble to three floor contacts, and ruled a foul for holding the ball more than three seconds. It was not until 1936 that the two division game with three forwards in

---

171) peach - n. (식물) 복숭아, 복숭아나무
172) misinterpretation - n. 오해; 오역
173) confusion - n. 혼돈, 혼란; 당황, 어떨떨함
174) edit - vt. 편집하다; 교정하다

one half of the court and three guards in the other was recognized by the basketball rules committee.

This basic pattern remained official for more than a quarter of a century. Throughout the years the sport has had a history of multipe and differing rules. In 1899 some players and teachers refused to accept the modification[175] of the men's rules. Today a limited number of teams play modified boys' rules rather than rules designed for women. A limited number of state high school athletic associations have independent rules, but the differences between their rules and those of the A.A.U. and D.G.W.S. are fewer each year.

Since 1905 there has been an active and permanent basketball committee that plans and revises[176] rules. Recently, in an attempt to bring A.A.U. and D.G.W.S. rules into agreement, a rule was changed to allow roving[177] players. This change made basketball more physically demanding and strategically[178] challenging and created more opportunity for general skill development among all players.

This committee remains the most active in team sports in

---

175) modification - n. 수정, 변경
176) revise - vt. 개정하다; 교정하다
177) rove - vi. 헤매다, 방황하다
178) strategically - ad. 전략상, 전략적으로

the Division for Girls and Women's Sports of the American Association for Health, Physical Education, and Recreation in its effort[179] to revise and introduce rules to make the game more interesting and to protect the health and safety of players.

Nature and purpose of the game

Basketball is played by two teams of five players each on a rectangular[180] court no larger than 94 by 50 feet. The court is divided into two equal areas so that each team has a front court, where its own basket is located, and back court, which has the basket it defends (the opponent's basket). Each team tries to get the ball and move it by passing, throwing, batting, bouncing, rolling, or handing it to a player who may shoot it into her basket and score a goal.

The team not in possession[181] of the ball tries to keep the opposing team from scoring as it tries to intercept[182], tie, or otherwise gain the ball and eventually make a scoring effort. The score of a team is the total of its field goals and free throws.

---

179) effort - n. 노력, 수고
180) rectangular - a. 직사각형의; 직각의
181) possession - n. 소유, 점유; 입수
182) intercept - vt. 도중에서 빼앗다, 가로채다

Facilities and equipment

The Court. Basketball is played in and out of doors with leather and rubber balls in many informal[183] settings; however, an official game is played on a rectangular court at least 74 feet long and 42 feet wide and no longer than 94 by 50 feet. There should be at least 22 feet of overhead clearance[184]. The outer court boundary line and center division line across the court width[185] are 2 inches wide. Where possible, the boundaries should be 10 feet from any outside obstruction[186]. A center restraining[187] circle with a radius[188] of 6 feet is marked by a line 2 inches wide in the center of the court.

The free throw line, 2 inches wide, is marked from a spot 15 feet from the center of the face of the backboard and extends 6 feet in either direction, parallel to the end line. A free throw circle 6 feet in radius is drawn from the center of the free throw line. The half of the circle within the free throw lane is marked in dotted lines. lines 2 inches wide are placed perpendicular[189] to each of the lane lines at

---

183) informal - a. 비공식의, 약식의
184) clearance - n. 치워버림, 제거; 정리
185) width - n. 폭, 너비, 가로
186) obstruction - n. 방해; 장해, 지장
187) restrain - vt. 제지하다, 금하다
188) radius - n. (원, 구의) 반지름; 반지름의 범위
189) perpendicular - a. 직각을 이루는; 수직의, 직립한

distances of 7, 10, and 13 feet from the end line of the court(3, 6, and 9 feet from the face of the backboard).

Backboards. Rectangular or fan-shaped boards are made of plate glass, wood, metal, or other flat rigid[190] material.

The white or transparent[191] boards, with white marking, hang 4 feet inside the court parallel to the endline.

Orange colored metal basket rings with nets attached hang in the center of the board with the rim 10 feet above the floor.

Ball. The leather or composition covered round ball is between 291/2 and 301/4 inches in circumference[192], weighs between 20 and 22 ounces, and bounces between 49 and 54 inches when dropped from a height of 6 feet. Balls of reputable[193] manufacturers meet official specifications. Each team of five should have at least two ball for practice.

Costume. The official gymnasium costume is satisfactory for most game situations. Attractive shorts and shirts which

---

190) rigid - a. 굳은, 단단한, 휘어지지 않은
191) transparent - a. 투명한, 비쳐 보이는
192) circumference - n. 원주; 주위; 주변(지역); 영내, 영역; 경계선
193) reputable - a. 평판 좋은, 영명 높은; 훌륭한, 존경할 만한

allow freedom are desirable for interscholastic and intercollegiate games. Footwear is an important safety feature. Each player should wear one or two pairs of light socks that cushion the feet and prevent blisters[194]. Basketball shoes with cupped soles are generally preferred over the tennis-type shoe.

In competitive games each player should wear a solid color number on her uniform. Slipover pinnies[195] are suitable with back numbers at least 6 inches high and front numerals 4 inches high. Both must be at least 3/4 inches wide. The single digits 1 and 2 should not be used. Combinations of two digits from 0 to 5 should be used.

Basic skills

Footwork, body balance, and ball handling are the foundation skills of basketball. A review of basic sports skills is helpful in preparation for game play.

Stance. A player preparing to more or receive a pass is in a slightly crouched[196] position with the knees bent and head and chin up; shoulders are slightly forward. The arms are

---

194) blister - n. 물집, 수포
195) slipover pinny - 머리를 꿰어 입는 유니폼 종류
196) crouch - vi. 쭈그리다, 몸을 구부리다; 웅크리다

relaxed and elbows bent with fingers spread comfortably at waist level. One foot is slightly ahead of the other so that the body is comfortable. Weight is distributed[197] on the balls of the feet.

Running. In running, the body leans forward as the knees rise to medium height. The arm action is natural and relaxed, and the arms swing forward to near shoulder height, poised to receive or intercept the ball.

Jumping. Development of leg force for high and accurate jumping is necessary for playing rebounds, tie balls, tipping, and shooting. Under the current rules one of the best offensive shots is executed from an extended jump position while the body is in the air.

Jumps may be made from one or both feet or from a skip step. With a push from the toes over flexed knees, the body "stretches out" high off the floor.

The landing is on the balls of the feet and the knees are flexed.

Catching. The type of catch used depends on the position of the ball, the position of opposing players, and the

---

197) distribute – vt. 분배하다, 배포하다, 배급하다

anticipated[198] move to follow. In preparation the arms are relaxed and spread upward in the direction of the ball. With the receiver facing the oncoming[199] ball, she steps forward to meet the ball with arms extended, elbow in, and hands extended. As the ball reaches the fingertips[200] it is cushioned into the fingers as the arms pull back slightly to "give" to ball momentum. The ball is caught by the fingers, thumb, and heel of the thumb, not the palm.

The hands are on the sides and to the back of the ball for all catches. When catching a high pass (above the waist), the thumbs point toward each other with fingers pointing upward. On a low pass (below the waist) the fingers point downward, little fingers pointing toward an imaginary spot to the rear[201] and bottom of the ball; thumbs are directed to the back and top of the ball.

Passing. A skillful basketball game hinges on effective passing to maintain possession of the ball. There are numerous ways of passing. The type used by a player depends upon the position of the body and hands of the passer and intended receiver.

---

198) anticipate - vt. 예상하다, 예기하다, 예감하다
199) oncoming - a. 접근하는, 다가오는; 새로 나타나는; 장래의
200) fingertip - n. 손가락 끝, 골무
201) rear - n. 뒤, 최후부, 배면, 배후; 맨뒤

Chest pass. The two-handed chest pass is the most widely used because it can be caught at chest height and lead to a speedy and accurate shot or return pass. The body may be almost erect[202] or crouched[203], with the ball at chest[204] level close to the body. Both hands hold the ball with fingers spread from the rear to the side, and pointing slightly upward. Thumbs are behind the ball with palms near, but not touching. Elbows are flexed and close to the body. The arms push forward from the shoulders as the ball is released in a straight line. As the ball leaves the hands, the thumbs give a simultaneous push and the palms turn toward the line of ball flight. The hands rotate inward on the follow-through as thumbs point downward and fingers extend in the direction of the pass. If it is not a deceptive pass, body weight should be transferred to the forward foot to give additional power.

<u>Two-hand underhand pass.</u> The "flip[205]" pass is not popular among girls except as a hand-off to a forward in a pivot play, or as a short pass when unguarded[206] in front.

The pass may be made off the front of the body or from either hip. In any case, the cupped hands grasp the ball with

---

202) erect – a. 똑바로 선, 직립의
203) crouch – vi. 쭈그리다, 몸을 구부리다; 웅크리다
204) chest – n. 흉곽, 가슴
205) flip – n. 손가락으로 튀김, 가볍게 치기
206) unguarded – a. 부주의한, 방심하고 있는, 마음 놓고 있는, 방어가 없는

fingers behind and on the side pointing downward; thumbs are on top pointing toward line of flight.

When passed off the front of the body, the elbows are flexed[207] and point away from the body more than in the chest pass. Feet are in side stride position. The arms extend forward as the elbows straighten, and wrists snap upward as the ball is released at waist height. The arms follow through low, with thumbs pointing up and fingers toward the path of the ball.

When the ball is passed off either hip, body position varies[208] slightly. To pass from the right hip the body is in forward stride position with the left foot forward. The hands draw the ball to the right hip so that the right elbow is bent, pointing outward from the body, and the left elbow is across the body with the back of the left hand resting on the hip. The ball moves forward with an arm extension and wrist snap as the body weight transfers to the forward left foot. The release and follow-through are the same as the "flip" from the middle of the body.

Two-hand shoulder pass. The two-hand shoulder, or sidearm[209], pass is useful at the completion[210] of a pivot, or

---

207) flex - vi. vt. (근육이 관절을) 구부리다; (관절이) 구부러지다
208) vary - vt. ...에 변화를 주다; 변경하다, 수정하다, 바꾸다
209) sidearm - a. ad. (야구) 옆으로 던지는
210) completion - n. 성취, 완성, 완결

as a deceptive[211] pass when the ball moves one direction and the body another. The pass may be made from either shoulder. The ball is held in both hands so the fingers and thumbs point upward and back and cover the sides and rear of the ball.

The elbows are flexed so that the right arm is close to the side and the left is across the front of the body. Feet are in forward or side stride position with the body rotated to the right from the hips and waist. The arms extend and wrists snap in a rapid movement as the weight shifts to the left leg. The body follows the ball as the arms and the hands extend and rotate inward as in the chest pass.

<u>Two-hand overhead pass.</u> This is a successful pass for skillful, tall players who are closely guarded or for any player who wants to release the ball quickly after catching a high pass. The ball is raised above the head, with the fingers at side and rear and thumbs beneath[212] the ball. The elbows are slightly bent and the wrists flexed. The body inclines[213] forward and the weight shifts forward as the arms extend and wrists and fingers snap to add thrust[214] to arm and shoulder power. The ball is released at a point in front to

---

211) deceptive - a. (사람을) 현혹시키는, 거짓의; 사기의; 믿지 못할
212) beneath - ad. (바로) 아래(밑)의, 아래쪽의
213) incline - vt. 기울이다, 경사지게 하다
214) thrust - vt. 밀다; 밀어내다, 밀어넣다

the body about head level as the hands follow the ball to eye level and turn inward, palms down and thumbs toward one another.

One-hand underhand pass. The underhand pass is effective from both sides of the body as a short, deceptive pass and a "feeder[215]" to a forward cutting to the basket.

The pass resumbles the underarm softball pitch. In executing a pass from the right side, the left foot is forward and body is comfortably crouched. The right hand is spread over the back of the ball and the right wrist and lower arm support the ball. The right elbow bends and leads the arm and ball past the hip as the left hand is placed on the ball as a guide. As the right arm starts forward the left hand moves away. The arm swings by the body and parallel to it, the arm extends, and weight transfers to the forward foot. The ball is released at waist height as the fingertips, hand (palm up), and arm follow the ball flight.

One-hand shoulder pass. The pass is much like an overarm[216] softball throw and is effective as a well controlled long or medium distance pass. To execute the pass the feet are comfortably spread and body weight equally distributed. The right hand is spread behind the ball so that it is supported by the fingers and thumbs. It is

---

215) feeder – n. 가축 따위를 치는 사람, 사양자, 비육가축 사육자, 선동자, 장려자
216) overarm – a. (구기) 어깨 위로 손을 들어 공을 내리던지는

brought back to the right shoulder by bending the elbow back and away from the body. The left hand comes across the body to serve as a steadying[217] guide as the body rotates to the right. As the body weight shifts to the left foot, the left hand leaves the ball. The right arm brings the ball forward, passing close to the ear.

The right elbow extends and the wrist snaps as the fingers thrust forward and pass under the ball, causing a slight reverse[218] spin. The throwing hand and arm follow through in the direction of the ball and end with palm down and fingers extended forward.

<u>Bounce passes.</u> One-and two-hand bounce passes are used for short passes in the scoring area, or any other place on the court when an opponent is between the passer and receiver.

They are often used on plays from out of bounds. For the one-hand bounce pass the preliminary[219] movements are similar to those of the shoulder or push pass, except that the ball is brought between the shoulder and waist on the right side of the body.

The left hand may balance the ball as the right hand is behind and toward the top with fingers extending upward.

---

217) steady - a. 고정한, 확고한, 흔들리지 않은; 안정된; 견고한, 한결같은
218) reverse - vt. 거꾸로 하다, 반대로 하다; 뒤집다, 뒤엎다
219) preliminary - a. 예비의, 준비의; 임시의; 기초의

The right elbow is flexed and close to the side. The ball is pushed to the floor so that it bounces and rises to a level at which the receiver can get it easily. The arm follows through toward the floor with palms down. If a waist level rebound is desired the ball should bounce 3 or 4 feet from the receiver. If a lower rebound is necessary, bounce farther from the receiver.

The two-hand bounce is executed much like the two-hand chest pass except that the action begins about waist height. The fingers are spread to the sides with the thumbs behind the ball.

The elbows are close to the sides as the ball is pushed toward the floor with a firm arm extension out toward the floor with a firm arm extension out toward a point on the floor. The arms rotate outward as the wrists and fingers thrust the ball away at waist level.

At certain times a spin is valuable with the bounce pass. On a long pass or when the ball must rebound close to the receiver with considerable momentum[220], top spin can be added by cocking the wrists back and then uncocking them vigorously[221] on the release. The ball leaves the small fingers first and the index fingers last. The hands follow through so that the fingers point toward the floor.

---

220) momentum – n. (기계, 역학) 운동량; 타성; 여세, 힘
221) vigorously – a. 정력이 왕성한, 원기 왕성한, 활발한

Backspin is used on short, relatively fast passes where a rebound up and away from the receiver is desired. The ball is released by a vigorous cocking action of the wrists toward the passer's body. The fingers release the ball after pulling upward and backward and the thumbs complete the action by pushing the ball down and forward. As the ball leaves the hands of the passer it is spinning toward her; the palms of the hands follow through, facing the spot where the ball strikes the floor.

Side spins are applied when it is necessary for the ball to bounce right or left hand to the right (under the ball) while pulling the right hand forcefully[222] to the left (on top of the ball). At the moment of release, the ball is spinning in a counterclockwise[223] direction. As the ball hits the floor it "jumps" to the passer's left. A reverse hand action results in a clockwise spin and a bounce to the left of the receiver.

Shove[224] pass. This advanced pass is also called the push-shove, or pass-volley and is an effective way of clearing the ball from under the basket or controlling a rebound or pass without really gaining possession of or "holding" the ball. As the ball comes toward the receiver, she pushes the ball toward a teammate by using one or both hands. The hands

---

222) forcefully - a. 힘이 있는, 힘이 든, 힘센
223) counterclockwise - a. ad. 시계 바늘과 반대 방향의, 왼쪽으로 도는
224) shove - vt. 밀다, 떠밀다, 밀고 나아가다

and fingers are firm and extended, elbows flexed. The wrists are flexed as the hands meet the ball. The arms extend and the wrists snap, giving direction to the ball. The palms and firm arms follow through in the direction of the pass.

<u>Hook pass.</u> The hook[225] pass is an advanced technique used effectively to return a ball to an inside court position when the player is held along the sidelines. For a right-hand hook pass, the body is in forward stride position, left foot forward. Initially the ball is held firmly by both hands at waist level.

The body turns so that the left shoulder is toward the receiver as the left hand moves toward the left side, leaving the right hand (fingers spread and pointing upward) and right forearm supporting the ball.

When a passer is standing or jumping upward, her right arm is raised sideward, so that it crosses the right shoulder and passes overhead, where the ball is released by a forceful wrist and finger snap.

The left arm remains extended for balance while the right hand pulls under the ball as it rolls off the fingertips. The hand (palm down) and fingers follow the path of the ball as far as possible.

---

225) hook- n. 갈고리, 훅; 걸쇠

Jump pass. This advanced pass technique is executed from an extended jump position while the body is in the air. Following receipt[226] of a pass, dribble, or rebound, the jump may be made from a stationary[227] position in which the player is standing on both feet or by stepping forward and jumping from one leg with the other following. The ball is held in position for either a two-hand overhead or one-hand push pass. If taking off from both legs simultaneously, the knees bend deeply and both legs thrust the body directly up from the floor. If the jump follows a bounce or dribble, one leg thrusts upward forcefully and the other immediately comes alongside[228].

Tennis

Although the French are often credited[229] with originating tennis, actually it evolved from a game played by

---

226) receipt - n. 수령, 영수, 받음
227) stationary - a. 움직이지 않는, 정지된
228) alongside - ad. prep. (...와) 나란히, (...의) 곁에; (...에) 가로(옆으로) 대어
229) credit - vt. 신뢰하다, 믿다, 신용하다

the ancient Greeks and Romans that is similar to modern handball. The English popularized an Irish version of the sport and played it on a court bounded at the sides by two parallel nets staked[230] down at the center so that each was shaped like an hourglass[231]. At first a hard leather, hair-stuffed ball was batted[232] between partners back and forth across a rope by their bare hands; several years later by a gloved fist, then with a glove protected by leather thongs wrapped around it. Later, a parchment[233] tambourine was used to swat[234] a linen ball, then a crude[235] short-handled paddle[236] was devised, and finally a racket and ball similar to those of today were used. It is believed that the word "tennis" is from the French "tenniz'" meaning "hold" or "take."

Early scoring was complicated with 15 "chases[237]" given for 1 point, from which arose the 15, 30, 40 game method of scoring. "Love," or nothing, which is symbolized by a zero or egg-shaped O, is from the French word "l' oeuf" for

---

230) stake – n. 말뚝, 막대기
231) hourglass – n. 모래(물)시계
232) bat – vt. ...을 (배트 따위로) 치다
233) parchment – n. 양피지, 모조 양피지
234) swat – vt. vi. (피리 따위를) 살짝 치다; (야구) 장타를 치다
235) crude – a. 가공하지 않은, 천연그대로의
236) paddle – n. (카누 따위의) 짧고 폭 넓은 노; 노(주걱) 모양의 물건
　　　　　　　(미국) 탁구의 라켓, (패틀 테니스의) 패들
237) chase – vt. 쫓다, 추적하다; 추격하다

"egg," pronounced by the English as "love."

King Louis X of France is responsible for the fact that tennis is called "The Sport of Kings." He jealously[238] guarded the game for members of his court and banned[239] the game for the masses when he found them playing it. In spite of the ban, the game became an activity for the "masses as well as the classes" and spread rapidly into England. It was during this period that a mesh net[240] replaced the rope and the crude racket, the tambourine.

The popularity of tennis swept out from England into the world. Major Walter C. Wingfield, a British army officer, did much to give the game impetus at home and in the colonies. Mary Outerbridge, a United States visitor in Bermuda, was intrigued[241] with the sport and returned to the United States in 1876 well supplied with rackets and balls. Although delayed several hours by customs officers while they debated[242] whether to permit her to bring such strange gadgets[243] into the country, she not only successfully introduced the game to Americans. Largely due to their efforts and their following among enthusiastic[244]

---

238) jealously - ad. 투기(시샘)하여; 방심하지 않고
239) ban - vt. 금지하다
240) mesh net - n. 그물 네트
241) intrigue - vi. ...의 흥미를(호기심을) 자아내다
242) debate - vi. 토론하다; 숙고하다
243) gadget - n. (기계의) 간단한 장치; 도구, 부속품
244) enthusiastic - a. 열광적인; 열심인

fans, the official governing body of this sport, The United States Lawn Tennis Association, was founded in 1881. By 1900 the Davis Cup Matches for international competition among men were established, followed shortly afterwards by the Wightman Cup Matches for women in the United States and England.

Nature and purpose of the game

Tennis is a game played with racket and ball on an indoor or outdoor court by two or four players. In both singles and doubles play the object of the game is to score points while preventing opponents from scoring. Points are scored by effective service and ball placement, which cause opponents to miss the ball, or to drive it into the net or out of the court area. The skill of the game lies in mastering serving techniques, offensive and defensive strokes and footwork, and game strategy. In competition a player strives to win points, games, sets, and ultimately a match.

The singles game is played on a 27 by 78 foot court. The area is divided by a net strung[245] tautly[246] across the court parallel to the base lines. The top of the net is 3 feet, 6

---

245) strung - string의 과거, 과거분사 vt. 끈(실)으로 묶다; 매다
246) tautly - ad. 팽팽하게 친(밧줄 따위); 엄격한, 간결한

inches at each net post, tapering[247] to 3 feet in the center of the court. Each half of the court is divided into a back and fore court. The fore court is further divided into the right and left serving or receiving areas. The doubles court is 41/2 feet wider on each side. In a doubles game the additional "alley[248]" area becomes valid[249] playing space only after the service.

Play begins as the server delivers[250] from behind the baseline and to the right of the center of the court. Serving from the right, she serves to her opponent's right court. Play between opponents continues until the winner of the point is determined. The server then moves to the left of center and behind the base line to serve and begin play for the second point. Serving positions are alternated[251] until the game winner is determined.

Facilities and equipment

The court used out of doors has a surface of grass, clay, concrete, crushed stone, asphalt, or other composition materials. Indoor play is on a wooden floor or on canvas

---

247) tapering – a. 끝이 가늘어진, 끝이 뾰족한
248) alley – n. 좁은 길, 소로, 샛길
249) valid – a. 근거가 확실한, 정당한; 효과적인; 들어맞는
250) deliver – vt. (공격, 포격을) 가하다, (타격 등을) 주다, (공을) 던지다
251) alternate – a. 번갈아 하는, 교호의, 교체(교대)의

covering. Markings on concrete and asphalt courts are painted in white or bright yellow. Dry or white lime is usually used to mark grass or clay courts, although cotton and plastic tapes stapled[252] securely[253] in the ground are favored in some sections of the country, especially for camp use.

The net may be made of steel or other metal, and of hemp[254] or cotton cord twine[255]. Although tarred nets are more expensive, they are almost a must for outdoor use and should be strung on a weather-resistant cable[256].

The official net height is 3 feet 6 inches at the net posts and 3 feet at the court center. The net is held down at the center by a strap not more than two inches wide. The band covering the cord or metal cable should not be more than 21/2 inches in depth at each side. The net for singles should be 33 feet long, for doubles 42 feet, and should touch the ground alone is entire length and come flush to the net posts at all points.

The recommended costume for this sport is a white tennis dress, sneakers, a white wool socks. White shorts and blouse are acceptable on most courts.

---

252) staple - vt. 고정시키다
253) securely - ad. 확실히, 확신하고, 단단히
254) hemp - n. 삼, 대마
255) cotton cord twine - n. 면을 꼰 (밧)줄
256) weather-resistant cable - n. 기후를 저항하는 케이블

Other necessary personal equipment includes balls and a racket with a well fitting cover and press. The racket frames[257] are made of wood, steels, aluminum, plastic, or fiberglass[258], and strung with steel, aluminum, plastic, silk, nylon, or gut. A maximum of 18 main strings crossed by 20 evenly spaced, lateral strings is standard and meets the specifications of the United States Lawn Tennis Association. Quality rackets have handles made of basswood[259] or Malacca, covered with fine leather, whereas cheaper ones have "leather" grips made of rubber, plastic, or imitation leather.

The racket should weigh between 12 and 131/2 ounces with a grip of 4 to 41/2 to 45/8 inches for women, and weigh between 11 and 13 ounces with a grip of 4 to 41/2 inches for those between 9 and 12 years. Above all, the racket should not seem too heavy when swung[260] vigorously back and forth for several minutes, and the grip should be small enough so that the hand fits comfortably around the handle.

Good balls are a must for all players, regardless of skill. Balls are manufactured under specifications of the United

---

257) frame - n. (건물, 선박, 비행기 따위의) 틀, 뼈대
258) fiberglass - n. 섬유 유리
259) basswood - n. 참피나무의 식물, 참피나무의 목재
260) swung - swing의 과거, 과거분사 vi. 흔들리다, 흔들거리다; 진동하다

States Lawn Tennis Association, which requires that balls have a uniform outer surface, be more than 21/2 inches in diameter, and weigh more than 2 ounces. Those meeting such specifications are packed and sealed in air-tight containers[261] and bear the mark of United States Lawn Tennis Association approval. "Seconds" are not always marked, although some companies indicate that they are slightly defective[262] by stamping out the letters USLTA. These cheaper balls are usually available at sporting goods shops on request and are suggested for beginners with a limited budget[263].

A backboard is the best opponent a player can have because it usually returns the balls. The best backboards are made of heavy beaverboard[264] or pressboard[265] in regulation half tennis court size, painted green with a white line 31/2 feet above the ground.

They should be located at the end of each court. A line 39 feet from the backboard and parallel to it should be painted on the area to indicate a court base line. Additional lines, 12 and 25 feet away, enable students to station themselves

---

261) air-tight container - 공기를 단단하게 넣는 용기
262) defective - a. 결함이 있는, 하자가 있는
263) budget - n. 경비, 운영비; 가계, 생활비
264) beaverboard - n. (천장, 칸막이용의) 건축재료
265) pressboard - n. (압축한) 판지

quickly for short and long rallying[266] distances.

Basic skills

Footwork. The ability to get around the court quickly, moving forward or back, to either side, as well as to shift body weight and position, is the prerequisite[267] to successful play. The knees should be kept relaxed and slightly bent, with body weight carried forward. Player should shift their weight to the forward foot (usually the one opposite the hand holding the racket), move into each stroke with full power, and move quickly around the court in order to play the ball in front of the body.

Jump rope drills are ideal for learning to push off from the balls of the feet as you start each movement, as well as for general warm-up purposes. Suggested patterns include:

1. Skip in place 25 times on both feet, 10 hopping from the left foot, 10 from the right.

2. Skip forward 10 times, 10 backward, 10 to the left, 10 to the right.

3. Skip on both feet in place facing forward, turn to the

---

266) rally - vt. (테니스 등에서) 공을 연달아 쳐 넘기다, 랠리하다
267) prerequisite - n. 선행(필수)조건; 기초필수과목

left and hop twice[268], return to place, hop twice turned to the right, return to place.

4. Move forward with fast running steps, skip backward, round in a circle, to both sides, changing directions suddenly upon command.

5. Repeat all four patterns minetically swinging a racket without skipping the rope, then with an actual racket.

The Grip. There standard grips are the Eastern, Western, and a modification of the two, or the Continental. Although there are certain values in all three, the one most commonly and most successfully used is the Eastern, for it permits easy free ball stroking.

The Eastern Grip. Shake hands with a racket held perpendicular[269] to the ground, holding the first two fingers directly behind and well around handle, with the heel of the hand at the end and the heel of the end and the index finger spread slightly apart, thumb extended.

The Serve. A correct serve results from a combination of the correct stance, ball toss, swing, and footwork. In movement it is similar to the overhand baseball throw.

---

268) twice - ad. 2회; 두 번; 두 배로
269) perpendicular - a. 직각을 이루는; 수직의; 직립한

The student stands sideways to the base line with feet spread comfortably apart, weight equally distributed, and the forward shoulder pointed in the direction the ball is to go. The racket is held in the Continental grip[270] (similar to the Eastern backhand with the racket shifted from one-sixteenth to one-eighth of a turn toward the forehand grip). The higher the point of contact with the ball, the better the serve is likely to be. The ball should therefore be thrown straight up into the air as high as the fully extended arm and racket can reach, above the head, and over the forward foot, and be hit a its maximum height when practically motionless[271], just before it comes back down toward the ground. As the ball is tossed into the air, the weight shifts to the rear foot. When the ball starts down, the racket is swung back behind the head and the whole body weight shifts to the forward foot as contact is made with the ball above the serving shoulder. On the natural follow-through the racket is brought down and across the body. The amount of spin put into the ball is determined by the angle of the racket and is largely a matter of individual experimentation[272] and discovery. Although this spin-type serve is often difficult to learn, it has so many

---

270) continental grip - n. 엄지와 집게손가락의 교차점이 오도록 꽉 잡을 때 V 자형의 각도가 생기는 그립
271) motionless - a. 움직이지 않는, 정지한
272) experimentation - n. 실험, 실험법, 시험; 실지훈련

advantages to the player who masters it that it is especially recommended to those students who are highly coordinated.

The straight, of flat, serve, in which the same footwork, ball toss, and arm motion patterns are used as in the foregoing[273] spin, or slice, serve, is best for those beginners who have average coordination or below. In this serve, the Western grip[274] is suggested: that is, hold the racket as though it were a hammer[275] being used to drive a nail into a board above one's head in front of the body. To get this grip, place the racket flat on the ground, reach, and pick it up without changing hand or racket position.

The Forehand Drive. Used most often in game play, this stroke is usually the most easily mastered. Stand sideways to the net, feet in a forward-back position, hold the racket in the handshake grip, and hit the ball with a fully extended arm and racket, holding the elbow well out and away from the body. Shift the entire body weight forward as the ball is hit.

The wrist should be kept firm and one should move into the stroke, hitting the ball in the center or "sweet part" of

273) foregoing – a. 앞의, 먼저의, 전술한
274) western grip – n. 테니스의 그립으로서 라켓면이 지면과 평행이 되도록 잡는 방법
275) hammer – n. (쇠)망치

the racket so that it travels swiftly in a straight line and barely clears the net. The follow-through should also be in a straight line pattern, and will be if the ball is hit at an imaginary 9 o' clock position and the racket swept on through to 3 o' clock without the racket head' s dropping lower than the wrist.

The Backhand Drive. Although similar to the forehand stroke, the backhand drive is often more difficult for right-handed players to master, whereas many left-handed ones will develop a backhand superior[276] to their forehand. Hold the racket in the Eastern grip[277], modified by moving it one-quarter turn forward, and hold the thumb behind the handle for additional support. Stand facing sideway, feet in a forward and back stride, knees relaxed, and bend forward at the waist so that the racket arm can swing freely back and then across the body at waist height. Hold the racket head perpendicular to the ground, contact the ball, shift body weight forward, and follow through in a straight line pattern.

The Valley[278]. Used primarily at the net and in the fore

---

276) superior - a. (보다) 위의, 보다 높은, 보다 고위(상위)의, 상급의
277) eastern grip - n. 웨스턴과 콘티넨털 그립의 장점만을 취한 합리적인 그립
278) valley - n. 골짜기, 계곡

court, a volleyed ball is hit either forehand or backhand before it bounces. The best grip is that used for the serve (the Continental), with the hand holding the racket moved about three inches from the end in a shortened grip. The stroke is a short, sharp, chopping[279] motion that causes the ball to spin. The ball should be well above the top of the net when volleyed, and the stroke used as an aggressive[280], sudden attack. The footwork and stroking fundamentals are the same as for the forehand and backhand, but the swing is shorter and the ball rebounds of the racket face more than it is stroked.

The half volley, in which the ball is "picked up" just as it bounces, is hit like the regular volley and is used to return a ball when in a tight spot at an unfavorable court position.

The Smash[281]. Similar to the serve, this stroke can be a forceful attacking shot of great speed. It is done using the same grip, footwork, and timing as the serve and is most effective when used on a high, weak return at the net or in midcourt. The player watches and waits, relaxed, until the ball drops toward the court. Contact is powerful with a firm follow-through.

---

279) chop - vt. (테니스, 크리켓) 공을 깎아치다
280) aggressive - a. 침략적인, 싸우기 좋아하는; 호전적인
281) smash - vt. (구기) 스매시하다, 강하게 내리치다

The Lob[282]**.** The purpose of the lob is to move the opponent around the court or send the ball over her head. It is a defensive time-gainer and should be placed strategically on the court. Played either on the forehand or backhand side, it is done by shortening and slowing down the backswing and lifting the ball with a forward upswing and follow-through as the racket, with the ball. This often effective, but delicate, stroke can send an aimed high and flatly hit ball into an unguarded area, and thus often becomes a sure point winner.

The Chop. The chop stroke is more defensive than offensive and is used to break up a strong drive or service. For both forehand and backhand chops the racket is held in a grip halfway between the Eastern forehand and the backhand.

A short backswing precedes a descending blow on the back of the ball with an open racket face. The downward and forward follow-through completes the action, which results in a ball that bounces short and low in the opponent's court.

The Drop[283]**.** The drop shot serves as a change of pace or

---

282) lob - n. (테니스) 높고 완만한 공을 보냄
283) drop - n. 방울, 물방울; 낙하; (온도 따위) 강하; (가격 따위) 하락; (낙하산에 의한) 공중투하

a deceptive stroke intended to place the ball just over the net and catch the opponent deep in the back court. Use a grip similar to that used for the chop stroke. The body faces the net more squarely than for a drive, and a short backswing leads the racket to the ball. The racket strokes the ball lightly so that it barely clears the net in the intended direction. The follow-through should be very short.

Game strategy[284]

The attacking style is usually played at the net with the defensive players moving back to base line positions. Although most players "beat themselves" through their own errors, this may be avoided by carefully analyzing all mistakes made and not repeating them. Consistent, steady play is more fruitful[285] than taking unwise chances, or trying to "kill" as many shots as possible.

Beginners especially should learn (a) to hit the ball away from their opponents, (b) to anticipate[286] where the returned ball will land on the court and be ready to receive it, and (c) to outsmart[287] their opponents by placing

---

284) strategy - n. 용병학, 병법
285) fruitful - a. 열매가 많이 열리는, 열매가 잘 맺는
286) anticipate - vt. 예기하다, 예상하다, 예감하다
287) outsmart - vt. ...을 압도하다; 속이다, 의표를 찌르다

returned shots to their weakness (this may be one of the doubles partners, the backhand of one, or the inability of both to move quickly around the court). Other aspects of general strategy include:

1. Return to the center line at fore or back court position after each stroke.

2. Conserve[288] strength by letting impossible shots go past and only going after those you can get.

3. Take your time and get into proper position before hitting the ball and play it in front of your forward foot.

4. It is not how hard you hit the ball, but where you hit it.

5. Always win your own serve and vary its speed and placement.

6. Hit the ball away from your opponent, trying to make her move around the court, from back to front to base line.

7. A deep cross court shot is usually much more effective than a base line drive.

8. Disguise your intended return as long as possible.

9. Play against opponents who are more skillful than you are, but remember to profit from what you have learned from each of these experiences.

10. Direct most serves to your opponent's backhand if this is her weakest stroke (this is often not true of left-handed

---

288) conserve - vt. 보호하다; 보존하다

players). Remember that the flat serve is most successfully placed when it lands in the backhand corner of the forehand court and also that the American twist serve is placed best when it lands in the backhand corner of the backhand court.

11. Vary the pace, spin, depth, and direction of your strokes in order to keep your opponent guessing and on the defensive. Master the art of anticipating what your opponent is going to do.

Doubles strategy

Teamwork[289] is necessary for success in doubles. Although advanced players prefer to play side by side, beginners should learn the up and back method, the side by side, and a fast shift to either one. Since the most advantageous[290] court spot is at the net, this position should be gained and held as long as possible. Other suggestion include:

1. Keep the ball in the opponent's back court as much as possible.

2. Make the opponents hit the ball up to you on their

---

289) teamwork – n. 팀워크, 협력
290) advantageous – a. 유리한; 형편이 좋은

returns by placing it at their feet.

3. Play the ball so that it lands halfway[291] along the base line until an open spot appears, then shoot quickly for this hole.

4. The server should come to the net after most serves if both partners are especially good net players.

5. Smash, volley, and lob as often as possible and keep sending the ball back into the far court.

6. Keep your opponent guessing and on the move by playing to their weakness and using a variety[292] of shots.

7. Make your opponent hit the ball up so you can hit it down on the return.

8. Keep attacking and moving in.

9. When all four players are at the net, drive the ball hard to the closet player; when both players are equal distance from the net, hit the ball so that it lands low down the center of the court or is hit to the weaker opponent.

10. Remember that in doubles most points are won from the net position.

Key phrases[293] in learning strategy are (a) play through your strength to your opponent's weakness, (b) anticipate,

---

291) halfway - a. 도중의, 중간의
　　　　　　　　ad. 도중에(까지); 거의, 거지반; 타협하여
292) variety - n. 변화, 다양성
293) key phrases - n. 강조하는 말씨나 표현

(c) keep your opponent moving, (d) change the pace, and (e) always change a losing game.

Archery

Archery[294] is a year-round sport for both sexes of all ages. Properly played either indoors or outdoors as an individual or group activity, it can improve posture and develop chest, abdominal, arm, and back strength as well as general physical fitness. Its carryover[295] value is among the highest of all sports, for a beginning archer may develop into a hobbyist who makes her own arrows and leaves the stationary[296] target for an occasional field shoot or a hunting trip.

This ancient sport of Robin Hood, William Tell, and Hiawatha[297] has strong romantic appeal, especially to youth. Archery's history began with primitive[298] men who

---

294) archery - n. 궁술, 궁도; 양궁
295) carryover - n. 이월품; 이월거래; 나머지
296) stationary - a. 움직이지 않는, 정지된
297) Hiawatha - n. Longfellow의 시에 나오는 아메리카 인디언 영웅
298) primitive - a. 원시의, 원시시대의

fashioned[299] the bow and arrow to protect themselves and to provide food. Its history contains the colorful panorama of Egyptian, Greek, Turkish, Japanese, English, and French armies with soldiers standing shoulder to shoulder or mounted on heavily padded horses shooting hundreds of arrows in union at the approaching enemy. Museums in almost every nation have exhibits of these ancient weapons- the shorter arrows, the oddly[300] shape C bow from which 6 foot long arrows were shot, the highly polished English or Oriental crossbows, the unattractive but deadly weapons of the Indian hunters, or the poisoned arrows of uncivilized tribes.

Since the beginning of the 17th century, after gunpowder gained prominence[301] as a means of warfare[302] in most of the world, archery continued to gain popularity as a sport. In the United States today more than 4.5 million people of varying ages participate in target and field archery in schools, colleges, camps, forests, and parks. For more than 20 years the Camp Archery Association has granted proficiency[303] certificates[304] to youth in Y's, schools, and

---

299) fashioned - a. (접미사적) ...풍; (식물) ...형의
300) oddly - ad. 기이하게, 기묘하게, 이상하게
301) prominence - n. 돌기, 돌출; 돌출부, 돌출물; 두드러짐; 탁월
302) warfare - n. 전투(행위); 교전(상태); 전쟁; 싸움
303) proficiency - n. 숙달, 연달, 능숙
304) certificate - n. 증명서; 검정서; 면허장

summer camps. The National Archery Association, organized in America in 1879, and the National Field Archery Association, founded in 1939, sponsor annual tournaments. The Division for Girls and Women's Sports of the American Association for Health, Physical Education, and Recreation sponsors an annual winter intercollegiate telegraphic tournament.

Archery is receiving additional emphasis clinics and workshops sponsored by the Outdoor Education Project of the American Association for Health, Physical Education, and Recreation.

Nature and purpose of the sport

The skills basic to the sport of archery are used in many archery activities. The most common form of target archery leads to the development of field archery, flight shooting, archery games, and bow hunting.

Basic skills

Many skills are basically the same for both target and field archery. Differences will be mentioned in the discussion that follows.

Prior[305] to developing shooting skills, the beginner should determine her dominant eye. Although shooting is done with both eyes open, the dominant eye aligns[306] with linear objects and consequently the shooting arm should be on the same side.

A simple method is to extend both arms in front of the body. The palms are facing away from the body and the fingers and thumbs overlap so that there is a small opening between the two hands. With both eyes open, focus on an object through the opening. Close the left eye; if the object remains in the opening, the right eyes is dominant. To verify this, close the right eye and see if the object moves from focus. Occasionally a person may have "nondominance" and she may then shoot from the most natural side.

Bracing and unbracing the bow. A commercial bow stringer is a common and desirable accessory. Not only does it lesson the labor of bow stringing for the individual, it also lessons or equalizes the stress on the bow while being strung.

The push-pull method is frequently used on light target bows. The lower end of the bow is placed against the inside arch of the left foot with the back of the bow toward the

---

305) prior - a. 앞의, 전의; ...보다 앞선, 상석의, 중요한
306) align - vt. 일렬로 세우다, 일직선으로 맞추다

body. The bow tip does not touch the ground but is pressed against the foot. The heel of the right hand is placed near the bow tip while the left hand, on the handle, pulls the bow toward the body. The heel of the right hand presses the upper limb of the bow down while the thumb and index finger slide up the bow and slip the noose[307] into the neck.

To unstring[308] the bow, the same bow, hand, and body positions are used. The string is lifted from its nock by the index and middle fingers and slipped down the bow as the left hand pulls the bow toward the body.

For a heavior or recurve[309] bow the step-in stringing method is often used. With the right leg between the string and the belly[310] of the bow, belly facing forward, the lower end of the bow rests on the instep of the left foot. As the right hand pushes the bow forward at the top of the upper limb, the bow forward at the handle bends against the back of the right thigh. The left hand guides the string into the nock[311]. Use of a commercial bow string for bows usually strung by the "push pull" method prevents twisting and possible damage to bow limbs.

---

307) noose - n. 올가미; (부부의) 유대, 결속, 얽매임
308) unstring - vt. (현악기 등의) 현을 풀다; …의 긴장을 풀다, 느슨하게 하다
309) recurve - vt. 뒤로 휘게하다 vi. (물길 등이) 굽이쳐 되돌아오다, 반곡하다
310) belly - n. 배, 복부
311) nock - n. 활고자, 오늬 vt. 활고자를 달다, 화살을 시위에 메우다

The stance. The target archer[312] stands astride[313] the shooting line, the left archer behind the shooting stake[314], with body weight equally distributed. For the right-handed archer the left shoulder and head are turned toward the target and the feet are spread shoulder width. The left foot is moved backward approximately 6 inches and the toe turns slightly to the target to complete the open stance. The body is held in a comfortable, relaxed, yet erect[315], position. The stance must be consistent.

The grip and bow arm. The fingers and thumb of the bow[316] hand lightly encircle[317] the bow so that the "V" of the thumb and forefinger is at the pivot point of the handle. The bow is held parallel to the ground and pointing toward the target with string toward the body until the arrow is nocked.

The bow is raised upright, and in preparation for the draw the bow arm is raised to shoulder height. During the draw and release, the bow handle is pushed by the "V" formed by the fleshy part of the thumb and hand. The forefinger is

---

312) archer – n. (활의) 사수, 궁술가
313) astride – ad. a. (형용사로는 서술적) ...에 걸터앉아; 두 다리를 쩍 벌리고
314) stake – n. 말뚝, 막대기
315) erect – a. 똑바로 선, 직립의
316) bow – n. 활; 활의 사수
317) encircle – vt. 에워(둘러) 싸다

174

around the back of the bow and the thumb may be resting lightly on the forefinger. The other three fingers no longer "hold" the bow but are relaxed in an extended position and point toward the target.

The wrist is straight and firm. The arm is comfortably extended with the elbow turned out, away from the bowstring[318]. The bow arm shoulder is kept down and back to avoid leaning toward the target.

Nocking. The bow is held horizontal to the ground with the cock feather up, the drawing hand, holding the nock of the arrow between the thumb and index finger, slides the arrow across the arrow rest and places the nock on the serving. A 90 degree angle is formed by the arrow[319] and the string. The thumb remains in contact with the arrow until the index finger and the other drawing fingers reach behind the string to stabilize[320] the arrow. Often the index finger of the bow hand may be needed to support the arrow until it is partially drawn.

---

318) bowstring - n. 활시위; (현악기 따위의) 줄
319) arrow - n. 화살
320) stabilize - vt. 안정시키다, 견고하게 하다

Drawing and anchoring. The first three fingers of the right hand grasp under the string with the fingertips[321] (no farther back than the first joint). The back of the hand remains straight, with flexion only in the first and second finger flexed during the draw. The arrow is positioned between the first and second fingers. At the same time the bow arm is raised, the drawing arm is pulled backward by the muscles of the back, shoulder, and arm. When fully extended, the right elbow is bent and parallel to the ground. During the draw take a deep breath and hold it.

Anchor point. Anchor point refers to the point on the archer' s face at which she places her hand when the bowstring is fully drawn. The point is often described as low, a point on or under the jaw[322] bone, or high, a point on or directly under the check bone. The anchor point, once established, must be used consistently[323] and constantly for all distances.

Target archers using point of aim or bow sight shooting usually prefer an anchor point under the chin. On each draw the string is drawn so that it bisects[324] the tip of the

---

321) fingertip - n. 손가락 끝; 골무
322) jaw - n. 턱, (특히) 아래턱
323) consistently - ad. 일관되게, 조리있게, 모순 없이
324) bisect - vt.vi. 양분하다; 갈라지다; (수학) 이등분하다

nose and the chin. The hand is anchored under the jaw and against the neck with the forefinger against the chin. Field archers, bow hunters, and instinctive shooters usually anchor at the back corner of the mouth. The upper surface of the index finger rests snugly[325] under the right cheekbone. Field archers often tip the upper limb of the bow and their heads 15 to 30 degrees to insure[326] that the eye is over the arrow.

Aiming. Point of aim and "bow sight method" are used by most target archers. The instinctive[327] method is gaining popularity and may replace the antiquated[328] point of aim method.

Point of aim involves using a spot on the ground, target, or background at which the archer sights over her arrow tip.

This point must be adjusted for each distance shot, bow weight design, and changing environmental conditions. For shooting long distances, the point of aim should be well above the target; and in front of it for short range[329] shooting. The point of aim should be lowered when arrows

---

325) snugly - ad. 있기 편하게; 조촐하게
326) insure - vt. 보증하다, 책임을 맡다; 확실히 하다
327) instinctive - a. 본능적인, 직감적인
328) antiquated - a. 낡아빠진, 안 쓰이는, 노후한
329) range - n. 열, 줄; 범위, 한계; 시계

go over the target and raised when they go below it.

After a point of aim is found for a specific distance, it should be recorded on a range finder for future use. A short stick or tongue depressor[330] can serve as a range finder when it is held by the extended bow arm in a shooting position with the top of the thumbnail matching a ground point of aim. The edge[331] of the stick is aligned with eye to the center of the gold.

When improvised[332] or manufactured bow sights are used, the center of the target is the point of aim, regardless of distance. The sight is attached to the back of the bow slightly above the arrow rest. The "pin" extends to the left side of the bow. If possible, keep both eyes open, allowing the "master" eye to sight the pin and align it with the gold. Correct settings are found by trial and error. If arrows group anywhere other than at the center of the target, move the sight in the direction of the error for correction.

That is, if the group is high and right, move the pin up and to the right. Aiming in field archery differs from the previously mentioned target techniques. The field archer sights with both eyes on the smallest observable point in the middle of the target. If the archer see the aiming spot

---

330) depressor – n. 억압자; 내리누르는 것, 억압물
331) edge – n. 끝머리, 테두리, 모서리, 가장자리
332) improvised – a. 즉흥적인

immediately above the tip of the arrow and the released arrow hits the spot, the archer used point blank aim. Shooting with the same equipment at a closer target necessitates[333] lowering the bow arm; at a farther target, rasing the bow arm. The difficult part of "instinctive" shooting is knowing "how much." This is learned through practice and acquaintance[334] with one's equipment. Many field archers and an increasing number of target archers learn through concentration and practice to adjust the vertical space between the arrow tip and the aiming spot by appraising[335] the distance to the target.

Beginning archers will find the "pre-draw-gap" method an aid in learning instinctive shooting. The principle of the pre-gap method is that it sets the shooter's arm on a plane with the target and in the proper position, so that at full draw her concentration can be entirely on the spot she intends to hit. After the pre-gap spot is established, nothing moves except the draw to anchor. This method presents the mechanics and develops the security[336] for learning instinctive shooting.

---

333) necessitate - vt. 필요로 하다, 요하다; (결과를) 수반하다
334) acquaintance - n. 지식, 익히 앎; 면식, 친면
335) appraising - a. 평가하는
336) security - n. 안전, 무사; 안심; 보안, 방위

Release. In preparation for the release the body should be relaxed, yet in readiness[337]. The fingers open smoothly to release the string and arrow. The right hand and elbow move straight back from the anchor position into the follow-through or afterhold position.

Game rules and scoring

In target archery there are various competitive rounds, yet all are governed by the same basic rules and scoring.

Basic rules

1. Archers must straddle[338] the shooting line.

2. Lady Paramount's whistle signals the beginning of shooting an end.

3. Archers must be three yards back of line when not shooting.

4. When a round requires shooting from several distances, begin shooting from the greatest distance.

5. An arrow leaving the bow is considered shot if the archer cannot reach it without her bow.

---

337) readiness - n. 준비, 채비; 용이; 신속; 쾌락; 자진해서 함
338) straddle - vi. 두 다리를 벌리다, 다리를 벌리고 서다

6. All shooting stops on two blasts[339] of Lady Paramount's whistle.

Scoring

1. Score values are: gold - 9 points; red - 7 points; blue - 5 points; black - 3 points; white - 1 point.

2. An arrow that cuts two colors is given the higher value.

3. An arrow that passes through the scoring face so it is not visible[340] from the front counts 7 points, if shot from 60 yards or less.

4. An arrow rebounding from the scoring face shall count 7 points, if shot from 60 yards or less.

5. Arrows in the petticoat[341] have no scoring value.

Scores are recorded by listing the highest values first. Each score is recorded; a zero indicates misses or hits outside the scoring area.

---

339) blast - n. 한바탕의 바람, 돌풍, 폭풍; (야구의) 맹타
340) visible - a. (눈에) 보이는; 명백한; 분명한; 뚜렷한
341) petticoat - n. (스커트 속에 입는) 페티코트; 스커트 모양의 물건(덮개)

Squash Racquets

The development of squash[342] racquets is a success story of sports. Originating among the debtors in Fleet Prison in England, it is popular today in many outstanding colleges and universities and "exclusive[343]" clubs.

Although its exact date of origin is doubtful, the parent game, called "racquets," was probably played as early as the 17th century with a small, hard rubber ball and a large, heavy bat. To this day a passageway[344] back of Fleet Street in London is known as Racquet Court, recalling the probable[345] site of early games.

In the middle of the 19th century the game was introduced at Harrow School in England. An outdoor game, it required a large court area. Impatient[346] students, tried of waiting to play on the one court, devised a game playable on a smaller court either indoors or outdoors. Experimenting with balls and bat type rackets, the students developed the game as we know it, giving it its name because of the "squashy" sound made by the soft rubber

---

342) squash - n. 테니스와 비슷한 구기
343) exclusive - a. 배타적; 양립할 수 없는; 유일한; 전문적인
344) passageway - n. 통로; 낭하, 복도
345) probable - a. 개연적인, 있음직한, 사실 같은; 예상되는
346) impatient - a. 참을 수 없는; 조급한, 성급한; 몹시 ...하고 싶은

ball as it rebounded from the walls.

From England the game spread to Canada and was brought to the United States in 1880 by the Reverend[347] James P. Conover of st Paul's School in Concord, New Hampshire.

Growth of the game was slow, and confusion[348] existed for many years over equipment and facilities. This confusion ultimately led to the popularization of squash tennis when Stephen J. Feron improvised a tennis-type ball covered with netting. With refinement[349] and changes both squash games grew in popularity when given an enthusiastic approval by the Prince of Wales[350] while visiting the United States.

As the popularity of the game spread, it centered in Philadelphia, New York, and other Atlantic Coast cities. Squash remained primarily a man's sport, with the greatest play in Eastern colleges and universities. Soon women college students, along with men, turned to squash as a sport for fun that did not require large team groups or arduous[351] training. In 1928 Eleanora Sears from Boston won the first women's national tournament. Squash racquets was one of America's fastest growing sports until

---

347) reverend - a. 귀하신, 존경할 만한, 거룩한; ...님(성직자에 대한 경칭)

348) confusion - n. 혼동; 혼란; 분규; 착잡

349) refinement - n. 정련, 정제, 순화; 세련, 우아, 품위 있음

350) Wales - n. 영국의 남서부 지방(웨일즈)

351) arduous - a. 힘드는, 곤란한; 분투적인, 끈기 있는

the 1930's, when winter activities and bowling captured sporting fancies[352].

Nature and purpose of the game

Squash is a vigorous racket game played on a walled court that resembles[353] an empty room with a high ceiling[354]. The game may be played by two players (singles) or two teams of two persons each (doubles).

The object of the game is to score points by serving and placing returns so that an opponent cannot make a legal return.

Today there are approximately 1500 courts in the United States, largely in preparatory schools, colleges, universities, Y.M.H.A.'s and Y.M.C.A.'s Unquestionably[355] a game for all, the appeal to beginners is the ease of learning basic skills; to the housewife and businessman, the physical workout gained by a short period of participation; and to the proficient[356] player, the mastery of the many skills. The relatively slow growth of the sport is due to limited court facilities and the expense of new court construction.

---

352) fancy - n. 좋아함, 애호; 연모; 취미, 기호
353) resemble - vt. ...와 닮다, ...와 공통점이 있다
354) ceiling - n. 천장; 내장판자
355) unquestionably - a. 논쟁할 여지없는, 의심할 바 없는; 확실한
356) proficient - a. 숙달된, 능숙한, 능란한

Game rules and scoring

The object of the game of squash rackets is to serve and hit the ball so that points are scored by your own efficient play or by playing the ball so that the opponent fails to return it in a legal manner.

Serve. The server or receiver is selected by a spin of the racket. Thereafter[357] loss of service goes with loss of point.

Each time a player receives the serve she may elect to serve from either box. She must then alternate until loss of point or until the game ends.

If the server delivers from the wrong box there is no penalty[358], but the receiver may demand that it be played from another box if she does not attempt to return it.

When serving, the server must stand with at least on foot in the serving arc, not touching the lines, and serve directly to the front wall above the service line so that the ball rebounds in the opposite[359] receiving court but not on the lines. After hitting the front wall the ball may hit the side or back walls, or both. It may be volleyed by the receiver, who does not wait for a floor bounce. Two attempts at service are allowed. If the first is a fault[360], the second serve is taken

---

357) thereafter - ad. 그 후, 그 이래, 그로부터
358) penalty - n. (경기) 반칙의 벌, 페널티
359) opposite - a. 마주보고 있는, 맞은 편의, ...에 면하고 있는
360) fault - n. 과실, 잘못, 허물, 실패

from the same side. When both serves are faults there is a loss of point and the serve passes to opponent.

Return of service and subsequent[361] play. To make a good return of service or any play thereafter, the ball must be struck on the volley or before it has touched the floor twice. After being hit it must reach the front wall on the fly, above the tell-tale. Before or after hitting the front wall it may touch any wall, but not the ceiling.

Scoring. A game is won by the player first scoring 15 points, except that:

A. At 13-all the player who first reached the score of 13 elects[362] one of the following:

1. Set to 5 points, thus an 18 point game

2. Set to 3 points, thus an 16 point game

3. No set - game remains 15 points

B. At 14-all, provided the score has not been 13-all, the first player reaching 14 points elects:

1. Set to 3, a game of 17 points

2. No set

A match is the best three out of five games.

---

361) subsequent - a. 뒤의, 차후의; 다음의 (일), 계속해서 일어나는
362) elect - vt. 선거하다, 뽑다, 선임하다

Hinder. It is the responsibility of each player to move on the court so that the opponent has a fair opportunity to see and play the ball. When a player fails to give this opportunity, a "let" or "hinder[363]" is called and the point is replayed from service.

Let. When a let is called, play is stopped and the point replaced. The following constitute lets:

1. A hinder

2. A ball breaks in play

3. After the first bounce the ball rebounds on or above the 61/2 foot back line.

4. A player refrains from striking the ball for fear[364] of injuring[365] the opponent.

5. A player is hit by a ball off the racket of her opponent which was not traveling directly to the front wall. (Note: In tournament play a ball traveling directly to the front wall and striking an opponent is considered loss of point for the person struck. Without a reference a let is generally accepted[366].)

---

363) hinder - vt. 방해하다, 훼방하다 a. 뒤쪽의, 후방의

364) fear - n. 두려움, 무서움, 공포

365) injury - n. 상해, 상처; 손상, 손해

366) accepted - a. 일반에게 인정된; (상업) 인수를 마친
　　　accept - vt. 받아들이다, 수납하다; (임무, 명예 따위를) 수락하다, 맡다

스포츠 잉글리시
Sports English

2008년 12월 31일 제1판 1쇄 발행

지은이/전유섭
펴낸이/강선희
펴낸곳/가림출판사

등록/1992. 10. 6. 제4-191호
주소/서울시 광진구 구의동 57-71 부원빌딩 4층
대표전화/458-6451   팩스/458-6450
홈페이지/www.galim.co.kr
전자우편/galim@galim.co.kr

값 12,000원

ⓒ 전유섭, 2008

저자와의 협의하에 인지를 생략합니다.

ISBN 978-89-7895-312-2 13690

가림출판사 · 가림M&B · 가림Let's의 홈페이지(http://www.galim.co.kr)에 들
어오시면 가림출판사 · 가림M&B · 가림Let's의 신간도서 및 출간 예정 도서를
포함한 모든 책들을 만나실 수 있습니다.
온라인 서점을 통하여 직접 도서 구입도 하실 수 있으며 가림 홈페이지 내에서
전국 대형 서점들의 사이트에 링크하시어 종합 신간 안내 및 각종 도서 정보,
책과 관련된 문화 정보를 받아보실 수 있습니다.
또한 홈페이지 방문시 회원으로 가입하시면 신간 안내 자료를 보내드립니다.